PRAYER TIME

*C*₃

CW01095531

Faith-Sharing Reflections on the Sunday Gospels

Robert Heyer, Editor

U.K. editors
Stuart Wilson & Joe Kennedy

James McGill
Jean Marie Hiesberger
Jane Eschweiler, SDS
Gloria Blanchfield Thomas
Bill Huebsch
Carol Gura

RENEW International
Plainfield, New Jersey

NIHIL OBSTAT
For the United States:
Reverend Lawrence E. Frizzell, D.Phil.
Archdiocese of Newark Theological Commission
Censor Librorum

For the United Kingdom:
Reverend Terence McGuckin, BA, STL Mlitt, DD

IMPRIMATUR
Most Reverend Paul G. Bootkoski, D.D., V.G.
Administrator, Archdiocese of Newark

U.K. cover design by Danny Curtin, cover photography by Andy Rafferty

U.S. edition:
Library of Congress Control Number: 2001118622
Main entry under title
PRAYERTIME, Cycle A
cm.
ISBN 1-930978-01-4   (paper, vol. 1)
1. Church year meditations. 2. Prayer groups-Catholic Church. 3. Catholic
Church Custom and practices. 4. Common lectionary-Meditations. I. Heyer,
Robert J.,
editor, 1933- .

Published by the Diocese of Westminster on behalf of
RENEW International, 1232 George Street, Plainfield, NJ 07062-1717
Web site: www.renewintl.org
Phone: 908-769-5400

Contents

Acknowledgments

The editor would like to thank:
Msgr. Tom Kleissler
Mary C. McGuinness, O.P.
Katherine Andrews

Authors
Jane Eschweiler, S.D.S.
Carol Gura
Jean Marie Hiesberger
Bill Huebsch
James McGill
Gloria Blanchfield Thomas

RENEW International Staff Members
Julie Jones, Dolly Bandura, and Kathleen Longo

Consultants
Fathers John Russell, O. Carm., S.T.D. and James M. Cafone, S.T.D.
Small Christian community members from the many dioceses who piloted
the sessions and offered comment and feedback.
Sharon Krause and Roberta Hazelbaker.

U.K. Acknowledgments

Editing the text
Fr. Christopher Bedford
Fr. Peter Wilson
Roland Hayes

Music resources
Chris Castell

Foreword

In January 2003, the Diocese of Westminster embarked on an adventurous programme of Pastoral and Spiritual Renewal which it called *At Your Word, Lord*. Its aim was to awaken the priests and people of the parishes and other communities so that they might recognise afresh the gift of ministry that God has given to every person by virtue of their baptism. The programme used many techniques to help parishes renew themselves but at the heart of it was the small faith-sharing community.

Faith sharing in small communities is a new experience for many people and it took some while for it to become a natural part of prayer in the diocese. It needs perseverance. It is a new adventure and needs time to grow. In the diocese over 20,000 people met in groups of between 8 and 10 people. At the beginning of *At Your Word, Lord* these faith-sharing groups met for just six weeks during the renewal season. Following a break, another season of six weeks took place. After every season many groups reported that they had grown as individuals and with each other into a community and their shared faith had deepened. Sharing faith at a deep level was certainly a challenge but it was also fulfilling and in many cases liberating. People were able to share experiences of living as a Christian in a way that they had never done before.

Of course when this happens, the people who make up the groups are reluctant to give up when the season of six weeks ends. So many groups carried on that we found we had to provide material for them. This was one of the hopes that we had for our programme. Our prayer was that these groups, once formed, would continue to have a life and vitality for many years to come. We have published this book to assist the many, many small faith-sharing groups that are now a normal part of our diocese.

PRAYERTIME: Faith-Sharing Reflections on the Sunday Gospels serves the whole of the Liturgical Year and can be used either before the Sunday or after it. This book is for Year A but we also publish volumes which can be used in Years B and C. The Scripture passage is usually the gospel reading for the Sunday and is not printed in our book because we want to encourage you to use your own Bible. We make suggestions about hymns which might help. Singing together is good and always remember that St. Augustine says "the one who sings prays twice." No faith-sharing session should ever finish without asking the question "how has the Word of God and the experience of those around me challenged me?" We hope you will make a response and try to live it out in the days that follow.

This book is a resource produced by the *At Your Word, Lord* Team, re-edited from the original text as produced by RENEW International. We are immensely grateful to RENEW International for permission to modify the original text of the United States edition for use in the United Kingdom.

One final word. Although the book has been produced by a Catholic Diocese, it is our hope that it can be useful to other Christians. The gospel is for all and our book is meant to serve the universal Good News of the love of God in Jesus Christ.

Stuart Wilson and Joe Kennedy
Joint U.K. Editors
(on behalf of the *At Your Word, Lord* Team)

PRAYERTIME, Cycle A offers a resource for faith sharing based on Scripture. Using the Sunday gospel of Cycle A as the focus, meaningful reflections, focused faith-sharing questions, related actions for consideration, and prayers on each Sunday reading are proposed as sources for nourishment, renewal, and inspiration.

Each group using *PRAYERTIME* needs to have a prayer leader who is familiar with the service and process. This leader should obtain the Sunday gospel of the appropriate service. A liturgical calendar is included in the back of the book to assist both leaders and participants. Also, the leader should prepare the copies of the music selection if this is chosen as the opening prayer. Appointing someone to lead the singing might be helpful. Suggested songs are listed, but groups should feel free to sing a song of their own preference. A list of music resources can be found in the back of the book.

The service is designed to be flexible in the time required. Depending upon the size and purpose of the gathering, the prayer time could take from ten or fifteen minutes to thirty or ninety minutes. If the meeting is the regular staff meeting or parish pastoral council meeting, the prayer time would be shorter. If it is a seasonal small Christian community meeting, the prayer time would be longer.

The leader is encouraged to be creative in preparing an appropriate setting for sharing and prayer, eliminating distractions as much as possible.

Prayer Session Outline
At the first meeting or whenever new participants attend, all are invited to introduce themselves and share why they came.

At other times, this time might be used for sharing the experiences that resulted from specific action decisions from the previous meeting.

Invitation to Pray
The leader brings the group together and allows a few moments to acknowledge God's presence.

The leader may begin with the suggested song or use the alternative collect prayer from the Sunday liturgy, prepare another brief prayer, invite a participant to pray, or use the following suggested prayer:

> Loving God and Father, we ask your blessing upon our gathering.
> Open our minds and hearts to hear your Word and to act upon it.
> Give us the love and compassion of Jesus and the enlightenment of
> your Holy Spirit as we seek your will. We make our prayer through
> Jesus and the Holy Spirit who live in love with you. Amen

After the song or prayer, the Scripture reading is proclaimed. This means it
has been prepared. The leader should foresee this and select a good reader
who will prepare. If necessary for understanding, the reader might give the
context of the Scripture reading in a sentence or two, so that all may appreciate the meaning of this gospel.

After the reading, the leader invites everyone to take a few moments to
savour a word or feeling or question that arises in each person as he or she
listens to the reading. The leader then asks those who so wish to share this
aloud.

Invitation to Reflect
The leader asks someone to read aloud the commentary or have all read it
thoughtfully for themselves. Each person then shares his or her response to
the Scripture. The questions may provide guides for this. The focus centres
on how one experiences the action of God's Word in daily life.

Invitation to Group Sharing
After this reflection/sharing, the leader continues the group sharing by asking the first reflection question.

Each person should then share his or her response to the reflection and
questions. The leader needs to bring each person gently into the sharing
and not allow one person to dominate.

Invitation to Act
The leader decides the appropriate conclusion time to this sharing and
moves on to talk about choosing a specific action. Each may choose an
individual action or the group may want to do a common action. The primary consideration should be in determining a specific action (group or
individual) that flows from the sharing. The actions listed are secondary
suggestions.

When choosing individual actions, the leader will ask the members to share their decision with the group. When choosing a group action, the leader will guide the group in determining who will take responsibility for different aspects of the action.

Ministerial communities or committees may decide their tasks at hand are their responses. However, the task at hand need not be their only response. The Word always renews and challenges us.

At the beginning of the next session with this same group, the leader should begin by inviting people to share briefly how they carried out their action responses.

Invitation to Closing Prayer
The sharing is concluded with prayer.

The leader or someone he or she invites is responsible for the closing prayer. Each service has a closing prayer; however, the leader or participants may want to add or choose their own closing prayer.

SMALL GROUP PROCESS

Small group/community sessions are a very important part of the parish's spiritual growth and development. These small gatherings provide valuable opportunities for us, the people of God, to share our faith, to listen more closely to the Holy Spirit, and to witness that God has called us, and continues to touch us and heal us as individuals, families, neighbours, and parishioners.

Understanding and respecting the ways adults learn is an essential part of small faith-sharing groups. It is important that the atmosphere be comfortable, warm, and friendly. Ambiguity and differences of opinion are to be expected. Each person is given the opportunity to express feelings and thoughts, examined in light of the rich scriptural tradition of our faith. Being accepted and listened to are essential ingredients of a good faith-sharing experience. There should be a true desire to listen to another's experience. A sense of humour is always helpful!

The leader/facilitator is the person who has the responsibility for guiding the group through the faith sharing and prayers (or assigning them to one of the members) of the small group session. Leaders of the small groups must be well trained for the task. By demonstrating charity and flexibility, a facilitator can effectively help the group to stay on the topic, gently include hesitant members, and develop a warm, accepting, open climate, and group cohesiveness.

Leaders do not provide preambles or prologues to questions; they do not frighten, shame, or argue with participants by word, gesture, expression, voice tone, or note taking. Participants may have questions about specific elements of our faith. Rather than trying to answer all questions, the facilitator may refer the questions to the parish team to gain answers about our faith.

A leader listens carefully to the participants and asks questions only when necessary to keep the discussion moving or keep it on focus. The leader needs to be prepared by understanding beforehand the questions and the background provided in the text. However, the leader need never be a slave to a set of questions or text, but should be able to adapt to what is needed for the sharing as it moves along.

When two or more Christians share faith, we are assured that Christ is in our midst and that the life of God and gifts of the Spirit of God are at work in us (see Matthew 18:20). Through the small group/community sessions, we are in a very vital way opening ourselves to the Spirit's working in us and through us.

Faith-Sharing Principles and Guidelines
In an effort to keep your group/community consistent with its purpose, we offer the following Faith-Sharing Principles and Guidelines:

Theological Principles
• **Each person is led by God on his or her personal spiritual journey. For us Catholics, this happens in the context of the Church.**

• **Faith sharing refers to shared reflections on the action of God in one's life experience** as related to Scripture and the Church's faith. Faith sharing is not necessarily discussion, problem solving, or Scripture study. The purpose is an encounter between a person in the concrete circumstances of one's life and the Word of God that leads to a conversion of heart.

• **Faith sharing is meant to serve our union with Christ, with his Church, and with one another.** With the help of God's Spirit, we contribute vitality to the whole Church. We receive authoritative guidance

4

from the Church's leadership; we are nurtured in the sacramental life; we are supported by a community of believers for our mission in the world.

• **The entire faith-sharing process is seen as prayer,** that is, listening to the Word of God as broken open by others' experiences.

Small Group Guidelines

• **Constant attention to respect, honesty, and openness for each person will assist the group or community's growth.**

• **Each person shares on the level on which he or she feels comfortable.**

• **Silence is a vital part of the total process of faith sharing.** Participants are given time to reflect before any sharing begins, and a period of comfortable silence might occur between individual contributions.

• **Persons are encouraged to wait to share a second time until others who wish to do so have contributed.**

• **The entire group is responsible for participating and faith sharing.**

• **Confidentiality is essential, allowing each person to share honestly.**

• **Reaching beyond the group in action and response is essential for the growth of individuals, the groups, and the Church.**

Advent Season

FIRST SUNDAY OF ADVENT

Stay Awake

Invitation to Pray
Pause for a few moments of silence and enter more deeply into the presence of God.

Song: "O Jesus Christ, Remember," Edward Caswall

Proclaim the gospel: Matthew 24:37-44
The Return of the Son of Man

Take a few minutes to savour a word, a phrase, a question, or a feeling that rises up in you. Reflect on this quietly or share it aloud.

Invitation to Reflect
Have you ever been waiting in a long line wondering what you could be doing, or even worse, should be doing? Just such a dilemma confronted the Church in the first century. Jesus was expected to return in "this generation." But "that generation" was nearly gone by the time the Gospel of Matthew was being written.

The return of Jesus was still expected, but the time of the return was unknown and becoming increasingly unknowable. It was as unknowable as the arrival of a thief or the onslaught of the flood in Noah's day.

What were the early followers of Jesus to do while waiting? Watch! Be alert! Be about the work of the gospel as if the Lord's return were to be any second now. A vigilance of waiting is superseded by a vigilance of acting.

We do not look for Jesus' immediate return with the same apocalyptic intensity of first century Christians. We have come to see over the centuries that God's transformation of humanity and creation is a more evolutionary process. We have come to see that we share this process with God. God will not do it without us. So while we wait, we cannot be idle.

As we begin the liturgical year, we seek to recommit ourselves to be a people who watch as we wait, who stand ready for the expectation of encountering the presence of Jesus who comes ever new into our hearts, our lives, and our world.

Invitation to Group Sharing

1. When have I experienced the coming of Jesus into my life at a totally unexpected hour or place?

2. How does Jesus' coming like a thief in the night challenge my need to be securely in control at all times?

3. How can we foster a sense of confident anticipation of Jesus' return without being either complacent or fearful?

Invitation to Act

Determine a specific action (individual or group) that flows from your sharing. This should be your primary consideration. When choosing an individual action, determine what you will do and share it with the group. When choosing a group action, determine who will take responsibility for different aspects of the action. The following are secondary suggestions:

1. Don't waste this Advent season. Stay awake. Make it a time to focus on Jesus who is always coming, whether we notice or not. Commit to spending ten minutes each day in quiet prayer as a preparation for Jesus' coming.

2. Practise patience in traffic, whilst queueing, with family members, in the doctor's office, etc. When trapped by circumstances and waiting with other people, notice them. Give them a smile. Pray for their needs. Extend a courtesy. Be gracious to them as God has been gracious to you.

3. Focus on being truly present to family, friends, or colleagues this week. Share the difference it made with the group next session.

Invitation to Closing Prayer

Give thanks to God (aloud or silently) for insights gained, for desires awakened, for directions clarified, for the gift of one another's openness and sensitivity. Conclude with the following:

| Leader: | In the night, |
| All: | Come, Lord Jesus. |

| Leader: | In the cold, |
| All: | Come, Lord Jesus. |

Leader:	As we wait,
All:	Come, Lord Jesus.

Leader:	As we tire,
All:	Come, Lord Jesus.

Leader:	Into our hearts.
All:	Come, Lord Jesus.

Leader:	Into our lives.
All:	Come, Lord Jesus.

Leader:	Into our world.
All:	Come, Lord Jesus.

Leader:	This Advent, we pray that we might wait in joyful hope for the coming of our Saviour, Jesus Christ.
All:	Amen, Amen

SECOND SUNDAY OF ADVENT

Repent

Invitation to Pray
Pause for a few moments of silence and enter more deeply into the presence of God.

> *Song:* "On Jordan's Bank," Charles Coffin, Tr. by John Chandler

> *Proclaim the gospel:* Matthew 3:1-12
> A Voice in the Wilderness

Take a few minutes to savour a word, a phrase, a question, or a feeling that rises up in you. Reflect on this quietly or share it aloud.

Invitation to Reflect
John the Baptist speaks the truth without fear. Such a person cannot be easily bought or threatened or coerced because normal society has nothing he or she wants or fears. Such a person can witness to the truth of the gospel. Such a person can point out what everyone else is ignoring. Such a person can focus attention on God's Word. Such a person can be a prophet.

And so John is. He is focused and his message is clear. It is stark and bold and unflinching: "Repent, for the kingdom of heaven is at hand!" (v. 2). Repent. It sounds like a call to "stop doing wrong." Perhaps. But perhaps it is a more radical challenge. John is not calling for external change. He is not saying, "Change your shirt." He is saying, "Change your heart; imagine yourself to be different; view yourself and others and all creation as God does; become who you were created to be. Do not settle for less."

Our response to such a startling call is often to back off and claim we already belong to that heavenly kingdom. Our dues are paid up, and we are in good standing. But John roars back, "I tell you, God is able from these stones to raise up 'good Catholics,' or 'born again Christians,' or 'children to Abraham.'"

True repentance is more basic than religious observance. All the prophets before John, and Jesus after him, talk about the necessity of knowing and loving God and doing justice toward one's neighbour *before* coming to the altar.

As Advent progresses, let the uncivilized voice of John arrest our premature holiday mood. Let his talk of vipers and axes, of water and fire catch us off guard and cause us to squirm a little. God must get our attention if we are to catch sight of the coming One who is "more powerful." For we will not see if we are not ready, and we will not be ready if we fail to repent. That is why God sends people like John. We may be uncomfortable with his message intruding on our festivities, but if we hear the message, we may be more open to the coming.

Invitation to Group Sharing

1. When have I felt truly repentant? Share some stories of repentance.

2. Who has been like John the Baptist in my life? How did I respond to the message of repentance?

3. What in this gospel calls me to look into my heart and see where the Holy Spirit is inviting me to repentance?

4. What can John's fiery preaching and strange demeanour have to do with my preparation for Christmas?

Invitation to Act

Determine a specific action (individual or group) that flows from your sharing. This should be your primary consideration. When choosing an individual action, determine what you will do and share it with the group. When choosing a group action, determine who will take responsibility for different aspects of the action. The following are secondary suggestions:

1. Recognise a prophet among the people you have read or heard about, or the people you serve, or the people with whom you work or live. Hear what God is saying to you through that person.

2. Take a specific time during Advent to be in an isolated place, even if for a short time. Do you sense God's presence and call in that place?

3. When you bathe or wash, feel the power of water to cleanse, restore and renew. Do you experience God's communication to you in that water?

4. Listen to the community you gather with as it seeks to prepare straight paths for Jesus. Hear what God is saying to you in those people and in their search.

Invitation to Closing Prayer

Give thanks to God (aloud or silently) for insights gained, for desires awakened, for directions clarified, for the gift of one another's openness and sensitivity. Conclude with the following:

Leader:	John, you scare us, but we ask you,
All:	Pray for us.

Leader:	John, you call us names, and yet we ask you,
All:	Pray for us.

Leader:	John, you make us squirm with your challenges, and still we ask you,
All:	Pray for us.

Leader:	John, you intrude on our festivities; nevertheless, we ask you,
All:	Pray for us.

Leader:	John, you are the very kind of prophet we need. You speak a word that rouses us. You speak a word that shakes us. You speak a word that empowers us by showing us the One more powerful who comes after you.

All:	Pray that we might welcome and announce such raw but loving Power unleashed to save our broken world. Amen

THIRD SUNDAY OF ADVENT

The One Who Is to Come

Invitation to Pray
Pause for a few moments of silence and enter more deeply into the presence of God.

> *Song:* "Wait for the Lord," Taizé chant

> *Proclaim the gospel:* Matthew 11:2-11
>   John's Question from Prison

Take a few minutes to savour a word, a phrase, a question, or a feeling that rises up in you. Reflect on this quietly or share it aloud.

Invitation to Reflect
It is fully appropriate that John's question is asked while he is in prison. The bound and confined questioner is in the best position and has the greatest need to look toward the future with hope. And this question, "Are you the one who is to come?" (v. 3) is asked with guarded but expectant hope.

Jesus is a sign of who we are called to be. He comes to us as we lie in prison buried, enclosed, cut off. We are stuck. Jesus comes to help us dig ourselves out.

What tools does he bring? He tells us: vision, mobility, hearing, life and good news. These are gritty realities, the material of everyday living, the substance of hope. And hope is the essence of the future.

The agenda of Jesus may have confused John who might have been looking for a warrior-king to destroy the power of evil and bring to bear God's judgment on a world in need of reform. Many of us would like God to fix what we have broken, clean up the mess we have made, and solve the problems we have created.

Instead of quick solutions accomplished by God, we get help from God and tools to fix and clean and solve. We hear about a process of salvation, not a sudden intervention. We discover in covenant with God and with one another that we are capable of becoming "more." Our eyes open wide to catch the first light. Our legs learn to stand after we have fallen. Our flesh becomes clean, slowly but surely. Our ears perk up to hear the distant sound. The deadness in us stirs and pushes against the entrapping stone.

In Advent, we wait for the One who is to come. He comes among us to share our struggle, our pain, our loss, and to say to us, "Nothing will be lost. Every striving, every hope, every impulse for life will have an effect. God remembers everything and everyone. Go tell John what you see and hear. You have seen the future. Let that vision sustain you in prison until the day of release. You have heard good news. Let that word of good news rouse you to life now and forever."

Invitation to Group Sharing

1. John asks a good question. How do I welcome "the one who is to come" (v. 3)?

2. What do I hope for—especially at this time of year?

3. What is the Good News Jesus brings to people who are poor? In what ways can I be an instrument of Jesus' Good News to those who are poor?

Invitation to Act

Determine a specific action (individual or group) that flows from your sharing. This should be your primary consideration. When choosing an individual action, determine what you will do and share it with the group. When choosing a group action, determine who will take responsibility for different aspects of the action. The following are secondary suggestions:

1. Consider becoming involved in some way with a local prison ministry.

2. Listen to someone attentively this week. Discover this person's hopes.

3. Good news is hard to find. Share some good news with another and be open to receiving the gift of good news from someone.

4. Identify a few of the gifts with which God has generously graced your community. Specify a way to use these gifts to meet the needs of those seeking sight and sound and life.

Invitation to Closing Prayer

Give thanks to God (aloud or silently) for insights gained, for desires awakened, for directions clarified, for the gift of one another's openness and sensitivity. Conclude with the following:

Father, you created eyes to see,
limbs to move, ears to hear, and life to be lived.
Help us to know our need for a word of Good News
that touches all our senses
and energises us to be a people of hope, a hope that trusts in what
is promised.

We pray this in the name of the One
who was promised and now is with us and for us,
Christ the Lord. Amen

Emmanuel

Invitation to Pray
Pause for a few moments of silence and enter more deeply into the presence of God.

> *Song:* "O Come, O Come, Emmanuel" (verses 5 and 6), Tr. by John M. Neale

> *Proclaim the gospel:* Matthew 1:18-24
> Joseph's Role

Take a few minutes to savour a word, a phrase, a question, or a feeling that rises up in you. Reflect on this quietly or share it aloud.

Invitation to Reflect
What's in a name? In the ancient world, everything. One's name was one's identity. And the one who names another is equally important. Here we see the Son of Mary receiving two names—two names revealed by God.

Joseph is the quintessential good person. His fiancée is pregnant, and he is not the father. He doesn't throw a fit and embarrass Mary and her family. He intends to quietly call off the whole thing. The angelic presence in his dream changes all that. Angels are prominent in the Scriptures to announce unanticipated changes in the lives of people. Angels tell forth God's surprises.

So Joseph is told to resist his instincts and go against the clear mandate of the Law. He takes Mary as his wife and legally adopts her son by naming him. He is told to name him Jesus. The name is not picked out of a baby book. "Jesus" means what it says: God saves us!

We learn that this Jesus will have a second name. This name, too, is revealed by God through the prophet Isaiah. Jesus is to be Emmanuel: God with us! (see Isaiah 7:14).

These two names tell us that this child will embody within human history the ongoing creative activity of God. God is always saving, transforming, recreating, reinventing, renewing, restoring, redoing. Jesus will be the lasting and fullest sign of this action of God.

And God is always "with us" and "for us." God is faithful. God does not change. God will be with us in the depths of our struggle and pain. Jesus/Emmanuel will be the greatest sign of God's fidelity (see Matthew 28:20).

As Advent draws to a close, we are caught up in breathless expectation of Jesus who by his coming, and more importantly by his staying, will show us how completely God is with us.

Invitation to Group Sharing

1. What does it mean when we say, "God is with us"? How is Jesus a sign of God with us?

2. I may realise intellectually that God is with me, but do I feel and experience the presence of God? Share insights.

3. How do I feel when God "surprises" me? Am I as calm as Joseph was and as quick to respond? How will I respond as a result of our prayer and sharing?

Invitation to Act

Determine a specific action (individual or group) that flows from your sharing. This should be your primary consideration. When choosing an individual action, determine what you will do and share it with the group. When choosing a group action, determine who will take responsibility for different aspects of the action. The following are secondary suggestions:

1. If they are still alive, ask those people associated with naming you how and why they decided on your name.

2. Open the telephone directory at random. Place your finger anywhere on the page. Read the name you are touching slowly and with reverence. Pray for that person, his or her family, and his or her needs.

3. When speaking to someone, use his or her name, speak it with reverence, realising each person is named by God.

Invitation to Closing Prayer

Give thanks to God (aloud or silently) for insights gained, for desires awakened, for directions clarified, for the gift of one another's openness and sensitivity. Conclude with the following:

Emmanuel—awaited by us.

Emmanuel—named for us.

Emmanuel—drawing near to us.

Emmanuel—living among us.

Emmanuel—being for us.

Emmanuel—God with us.

Come, and be born in our hearts!

Offer one another a sign of peace or a word of encouragement.

Christmas Season

THE HOLY FAMILY OF JESUS, MARY AND JOSEPH

Survival

Invitation to Pray

Pause for a few moments of silence and enter more deeply into the presence of God.

> *Song:* "Once in Royal David's City," (verses 4 and 6) Mrs C F Alexander

> *Proclaim the gospel*: Matthew 2:13-15, 19-23
> The Flight into Egypt

Take a few minutes to savour a word, a phrase, a question, or a feeling that rises up in you. Reflect on this quietly or share it aloud.

Invitation to Reflect

It takes many things to hold a family together: hard work, commitment, love, and trust—to name a few. It is tough and many threats present themselves over the course of a lifetime. So many things come upon us, from health and financial problems to strains in the very relationships that ought to bind the family together.

Then sometimes truly monstrous threats rear their heads. Death-dealing dangers arise and completely blot out any sense of value or purpose. The family is overwhelmed as catastrophe circles round.

Joseph and Mary and Jesus faced such a dilemma. Like countless families down through the centuries, they were uprooted from their home and driven into a foreign land because "death squads" were after them and others.

Long before Jesus faced the cross, Mary and Joseph faced it for him. They scrambled to hide him and protect him. The dangers Jesus faced as a young child, Mary and Joseph faced, too. They knew the fear and horror of being helpless in the face of violent power bent on destroying innocent life. Perhaps the lessons they learned they taught to their son.

Alerted by the angel's message, they flee to restart their lives first in Egypt and finally in Nazareth. How hard it is to start over again and again. How difficult to wonder if this is the final move. How scary to worry if the threat is really past—or only delayed!

The Holy Family faced such concerns as families have done throughout human history. Life is fragile and vulnerable at every turn. Life must be guarded and nurtured and strengthened. And yet, the only life worth living is a life lived at risk for another, a life that is given away, a life that is never fully one's own.

Jesus learned from the self-risking lives of his parents that the road to Nazareth was the same road that led to Calvary.

Invitation to Group Sharing

1. Have I ever felt my life was literally at risk because of a circumstance in which I found myself? In what ways did I call upon God or others to help me?

2. Share a time or an experience when your family and you had to move and restart life in a new setting. How did others welcome or receive you?

3. Our country has received many refugees in recent years. Do I know anyone in my community who has been uprooted because of economic, political, or religious persecution? If so, what is being done to support that person or family? What can I do to be supportive?

Invitation to Act

Determine a specific action (individual or group) that flows from your sharing. This should be your primary consideration. When choosing an individual action, determine what you will do and share it with the group. When choosing a group action, determine who will take responsibility for different aspects of the action. The following are secondary suggestions:

1. Get involved with a ministry that serves the needs of homeless families or refugee families. Listen to their stories.

2. Learn more about a specific unjust situation. Respond in some way, such as letting your elected representatives know what you

have learned and how you feel about the situation.

3. Reach out to new arrivals and help them settle in your community. Refer them to doctors, legal advisers, hospitals, churches, clinics, and so forth.

4. Become more aware of how human life is threatened in our society, for example, abortion, crime, poverty, nursing home abuse, latchkey children, teenage isolation. Decide what kind of response you will make.

Invitation to Closing Prayer

Give thanks to God (aloud or silently) for insights gained, for desires awakened, for directions clarified, for the gift of one another's openness and sensitivity. Conclude with the following:

Joseph, you led your young family from your house to a strange land as you fled death and violence. Pray for us when we must step into the unknown in order to preserve or defend our families.

Mary, you comforted Jesus and strengthened Joseph as you held your family together in the midst of confusion and fear. Pray for us when we face difficulties that rise up suddenly to threaten our families.

Jesus, you joined us in this life and ran all the risks we do and experienced yourself as vulnerable and weak. Fill us with your power so we will live our lives in solidarity with you and our families. Amen

THE BLESSED VIRGIN MARY, MOTHER OF GOD

The First Disciple

Invitation to Pray
Pause for a few moments of silence and enter more deeply into the presence of God.

> ***Song:*** "As I Kneel Before You," Maria Parkinson
> ***Proclaim the gospel:*** Luke 2:16-21
> Shepherds at the Manger

Take a few minutes to savour a word, a phrase, a question, or a feeling that rises up in you. Reflect on this quietly or share it aloud.

Invitation to Reflect
Among all the comments made about Mary in the New Testament, this one describing her as one who treasures all these words and ponders them is quite distinctive. It is not unusual that new mothers, sometimes immediately or sometimes when they regain some strength and the opportunity to reflect a bit, will treasure and ponder the wonder of the new life brought into the world. They will recall years later what family members or friends said about the new child.

Mary hears from the shepherds their tale—a story of angels and heavenly song and prophecy. The birth of this child, they say, is good news not only for her and Joseph but also "for all the people" (Luke 2:10). What a message to treasure and ponder.

The ultimate destiny and meaning of Mary's infant child will become more clear to her. Like many mothers, she treasures this child and ponders on what is still to come.

We honour Mary as the Mother of God. But in some ways her greatest "honour" is that she is the first disciple of her son. Her response to the angel Gabriel, "May it be done to me according to your word" (Luke 1:38), is the decision of a disciple choosing to obey and follow. As disciple, she has a unique role to play. She is to be the Mother of the Messiah, the Mother of Emmanuel, the Mother of God. Her "yes" sets her on the way to becoming mother. She is disciple first, then mother.

She treasures her choosing that has taken flesh in her Son, Jesus. And she ponders what it may mean to follow and obey this same Son.

Perhaps we share Mary's moment. We treasure the wonder of God's love revealed in the birth of her son. We also ponder what it means to follow and be changed by such a love.

Invitation to Group Sharing

1. How do I give flesh to the presence of God by what I choose? By how I live?

2. What does 'pondering' mean to me? Share something you have been pondering for a while.

3. Who are the unlikely 'shepherds' in our lives who are announcing the surprising actions of God?

4. How can we help those to whom we minister understand their experiences of how God is touching their lives?

Invitation to Act

Determine a specific action (individual or group) that flows from your sharing. This should be your primary consideration. When choosing an individual action, determine what you will do and share it with the group. When choosing a group action, determine who will take responsibility for different aspects of the action. The following are secondary suggestions:

1. Ask a new mother what she treasures and ponders regarding her child. Listen carefully to her.

2. Renew your commitment to be a disciple of Mary's son. What specific actions for you flow from that commitment to discipleship? Act on one.

3. Pray the Angelus daily (see back of this book). Contemplate the courage and tenacity of Mary as disciple and mother.

Invitation to Closing Prayer
Give thanks to God (aloud or silently) for insights gained, for desires awakened, for directions clarified, for the gift of one another's openness and sensitivity. Conclude with the following:

Pray together slowly, pausing at each phrase for several seconds to allow an image to surface.

>Mary, pray that we might treasure life
>beauty
>goodness
>opportunity
>truth.
>
>Mary, pray that we might ponder
>how to defend life
>how to see and hear beauty
>how to affirm and share goodness
>how to grasp and utilise opportunity
>how to seek and proclaim truth.
>
>Mary, pray that we treasure what we have and ponder on what we might become. Amen

Conclude with the Hail Mary.

SECOND SUNDAY AFTER CHRISTMAS

Mystery of the Incarnation

Invitation to Pray
Pause for a few moments of silence and enter more deeply into the presence of God.

>*Song:* "Joy to the World," Isaac Watts

>*Proclaim the gospel:* John 1:1-18
>The Prologue

Take a few minutes to savour a word, a phrase, a question, or a feeling that rises up in you. Reflect on this quietly or share it aloud.

Invitation to Reflect
The Prologue of John's Gospel always seems a little out of place during the Christmas season. There are no shepherds or magi or angels. There is no Christmas "story." Still, Jesus, the Word made flesh, is what lies at the heart of the Christmas Season.

The Word is described here as the means of God's power to create. The Word is the source of life and light. And yet this Word, who is Creator, becomes creature. The Word whose breath turns dust into living beings, becomes dust. This is such a great mystery that one must be repeatedly initiated into its meaning.

The Word made flesh is the place where God and humanity meet. This Word is the common ground where God and humanity can stand both open and vulnerable to each other. This Word is the common language that both God and humanity speak. The Word made flesh is God's self-emptying love extended and offered to creation and, at the same time and in the same place, the Word is humanity's faithful and trusting response to that love.

In the history of Israel, God was 'made flesh' in action (the exodus), in covenant (Torah), in poetry (the prophets), and in worship (temple and priesthood). While most of their neighbours believed they had to make contact with their gods in mythic realms, Israel experienced God as an initiator, an actor in creation and human history.

29

The Bible is perhaps the only great spiritual text where the principal event is not humanity's search for God, but God's search for humanity. From Abraham to Paul, it is God who makes the first move. And that move is almost always unexpected, unannounced, and unwelcome.

So it goes. The Word becomes flesh and is seen by all around. At first we are mildly curious about this newcomer. But the more we see and hear, we discover that this Word brings the fullness of life, the light of glory, and the grace and truth of the Creator God who will not stay away, who has fallen in love with what he has made. The Word made flesh has made this unseen love known. The Christmas story indeed!

Invitation to Group Sharing

1. How have I experienced a creative moment of God in my life?

2. How would I explain to someone that the Prologue of John's Gospel is a Christmas story?

3. What does the mystery of the Incarnation mean in my daily life? How can I live out its implications more fully?

4. What are some specific ways in which we can acknowledge and celebrate the goodness of creation?

Invitation to Act

Determine a specific action (individual or group) that flows from your sharing. This should be your primary consideration. When choosing an individual action, determine what you will do and share it with the group. When choosing a group action, determine who will take responsibility for different aspects of the action. The following are secondary suggestions:

1. Spend some time looking at your own flesh—your hands, your face, your body. Reflect on the sacredness of what you see, despite the difficulty in sometimes seeing your own flesh as sacred.

2. Listen for that unexpected and unannounced call from God. Spend ten minutes in quiet prayer each day this week, seeking to be open to God's call.

3. Learn more about how Judaism has a profound incarnational sense of God present in creation and history. Connect this with

the understanding of the Word made flesh.

4. Reach out to another person and share what the mystery of the Incarnation means to you. Listen to his or her insights about the Incarnation.

5. Think about your words becoming flesh. Use words that 'create life' this week.

Invitation to Closing Prayer
Give thanks to God (aloud or silently) for insights gained, for desires awakened, for directions clarified, for the gift of one another's openness and sensitivity. Conclude with the following:

Jesus, Word of God,
who has become flesh for our sakes,
help us celebrate the dignity of our humanity.
We are made in the image of God.
God chose our humanity
as the place of greatest intimacy with creation.
Help us share in this in-dwelling, liberating love,
and let us proclaim your presence
as Word of God among us. Amen

THE EPIPHANY OF THE LORD

Jewish Roots of Gentile Faith

Invitation to Pray
Pause for a few moments of silence and enter more deeply into the presence of God.

> *Song:* "We Three Kings of Orient Are," John H. Hopkins, Jr.

> *Proclaim the gospel:* Matthew 2:1-12
> The Coming of the Magi

Take a few minutes to savour a word, a phrase, a question, or a feeling that rises up in you. Reflect on this quietly or share it aloud.

Invitation to Reflect
Wise men? Kings? Astrologers? Who are these people? In the long run, it probably doesn't matter. They are Magi. They are searchers. They are observers of the night sky and the forces of nature. They are people not afraid to get up and follow their instincts and hunches about where the divine is calling them.

The star leads the Magi to Bethlehem but finding Jesus is not so direct or immediate. To find Jesus, one must encounter the peculiar activity of God revealed in the lived experience of Israel's history and found in the Torah, the Prophets, and the Wisdom writings. The star's rising leads them not to Jesus, but to Micah 5:1 and 2 Samuel 5:2, Scripture that speaks of Jesus' coming.

The Gentile Magi must immerse themselves in the atmosphere of Jerusalem and the history of Israel found there, or they will never discover the King of the Jews. Jesus is Jewish and everything he says and does finds its meaning in the light of what Israel already knows God to be doing and saying. It is difficult to find Jesus or understand who he is until one has encountered the God of the exodus, the prophets, and the psalms.

So the Magi sojourn in Jerusalem where they are enlightened. Then the star takes on a new meaning. It is no longer simply an object in the night sky, but the star that "shall advance from Jacob" (Numbers 24:17). Now the star is a true guide to Jesus. They pay homage and offer gifts.

But not all who read the Law and the Prophets see Jesus as worthy of homage and gifts. The King of the Jews who will proclaim the kingdom of God will be seen by some as threatening the 'kingdoms' that are already here. There is no room for another kingdom, especially one calling for an end to violence and greed and one promoting the justice and reconciliation of the Torah or Law. So while the Magi do homage, others plot murder.

This same choice lies before stargazers and Bible readers even today. It is not about stars or words on a page. It is about hearts open to God's transformation grace or hearts hardened around limited self-interests. The Magi chose. How do we choose?

Invitation to Group Sharing

1. When have I been moved to action by a star, a dream, a hunch, a vision, an impulse?

2. To whom would I go a great distance to bring a gift? Why?

3. When have I seen Jesus present in ordinary events and people in my life? Share some examples.

4. In what concrete ways can I encourage another's desire, dream, or vision?

Invitation to Act

Determine a specific action (individual or group) that flows from your sharing. This should be your primary consideration. When choosing an individual action, determine what you will do and share it with the group. When choosing a group action, determine who will take responsibility for different aspects of the action. The following are secondary suggestions:

1. Go outside on a clear night and look at the winter sky. Note the mystery and beauty of the cosmos spread above you. Give thanks to God, the source of that mystery and beauty.

2. If there is someone you would like to see who lives at a distance, consider taking a trip to visit him or her. Share the good news in your life.

3. Reach out to someone of another faith or culture or race. Cross the same barrier that the Magi had to cross in order to find Jesus.

Invitation to Closing Prayer
Give thanks to God (aloud or silently) for insights gained, for desires awakened, for directions clarified, for the gift of one another's openness and sensitivity. Conclude with the following:

You Magi, pray that we might see God revealed in the cosmos as you did.

You Searchers, pray that we might act on what we see and move into the unknown, full of wonder as you did.

You Questioners, pray that we might pore over our tradition seeking to appreciate anew what has been handed down to us, so that we might experience the wonder of the new life with God in Christ.

You Faithful Ones, pray that we might pursue the star in our lives as you did until it leads us to the Christ who is God-with-us.

You Listeners to Angels, pray that we might resist evil as you did and not co-operate in the violence and cruelty that attempt to destroy the life and love of God present among us.

You Magi, pray for us who seek Christ in wonder, majesty, and awe as you did.

Amen

THE BAPTISM OF THE LORD

The Voice of God

Invitation to Pray

Pause for a few moments of silence and enter more deeply into the presence of God.

    Song: "Water of Life," Stephen Dean

    Proclaim the gospel: Matthew 3:13-17
                         The Baptism of Jesus

Take a few minutes to savour a word, a phrase, a question, or a feeling that rises up in you. Reflect on this quietly or share it aloud.

Invitation to Reflect

Jesus' adult ministry begins with his baptism. Without a doubt, his baptism was a defining moment in the life of Jesus. He emerges from years of obscurity to become a public figure at the baptism.

Jesus came to be baptised, but does not need to be baptised. The paradox of who Jesus is begins early in his public life.

The circumstances following his baptism suggest that something momentous is happening in this experience. The heavens are opened. The veil that separates the heavenly realm from the earthly is pulled back. The gap between God and creation is shortened.

At the baptism of Jesus, the life-giving Spirit/breath of God that creates anew. The life-giving Spirit/breath descends not in the physical shape of a dove, but descends like a dove. It is not a literal description. God's Spirit/breath hovers over and gently envelops Jesus. Through Jesus' own death and resurrection, this same Spirit/breath will 'fire up' his disciples and through them the whole world.

Next the heavenly voice is heard, or better, overheard through the torn fabric of the cosmos. The voice speaks in heaven, but echoes to earth. For the end time, there were some who felt that God's voice would be heard directly and not mediated by prophet or sage. And so it *is* heard at the baptism of Jesus.

And what is heard is truly amazing. This Jesus is the Son, the Beloved, the One pleasing to God. This otherwise unknown person sees himself and is seen by others to embody the essence of God's reality on earth.

Our baptism parallels this inaugural event in Jesus' life. Having been plunged into the death-dealing waters, we arise made new and whole. We are transformed. The barrier between ourselves and God, a barrier established by sin and death is spanned. With Jesus, we are surrounded by the warm, brooding, life-giving Spirit/breath of God. And the voice echoes in us that we are known and loved by the One from whom all things come. With Jesus, we emerge from baptism empowered to do battle with our demons (see Matthew 4:1-11), and to become persons through whom God's life and love can be carried into the world.

Invitation to Group Sharing

1. When have I stepped forward publicly, as Jesus did, as a way of announcing and choosing a new direction for my life?

2. How does God 'speak' to me? Where does the voice of God echo in my life?

3. What can I do to live out my baptismal commitment more openly and fully? Try to be specific.

Invitation to Act

Determine a specific action (individual or group) that flows from your sharing. This should be your primary consideration. When choosing an individual action, determine what you will do and share it with the group. When choosing a group action, determine who will take responsibility for different aspects of the action. The following are secondary suggestions:

1. Learn more about the Rite of Christian Initiation of Adults (RCIA) process in the Diocese. If possible, pray for a specific candidate or catechumen throughout the process. Tell the person you are praying for him or her.

2. Become more involved in your parish Initiation process as a sponsor, godparent, or catechist.

3. Listen attentively to the voices of people in your life through whom the voice of God is echoing. Share with them how they are the voice of God for you.

4. Encourage someone who has intentionally changed his or her life for the better.

Invitation to Closing Prayer

Give thanks to God (aloud or silently) for insights gained, for desires awakened, for directions clarified, for the gift of one another's openness and sensitivity. Conclude with the following:

O Father,

May we come to life in the challenging waters of baptism.

May we find breath in the brooding Spirit enveloping us.

May we hear your heavenly voice call us by name and bestow on us your favour and dignity.

May we become a new creation filled with vulnerable power.

May we go forth renewed as your sons and daughters.

Amen

Lenten Season

FIRST SUNDAY OF LENT

To Be Tempted

Invitation to Pray
Pause for a few moments of silence and enter more deeply into the presence of God.

> *Song:* 'Forty Days and Forty Nights" G H Smyttan & Francis Pott
> *Proclaim the gospel*: Matthew 4:1-11
>   Temptation of Jesus

Take a few minutes to savour a word, a phrase, a question, or a feeling that rises up in you. Reflect on this quietly or share it aloud.

Invitation to Reflect
Jesus went into the desert and was tempted. It often happens that when we are alone, we, too, are tempted. Those thoughts, ideas, inclinations that we could call temptations can seem to come to us in the midst of quiet, sometimes when we least expect. There we struggle with our own demons. We might be alone, reflecting on the day or just remembering an incident that occurred and there, in that quiet, our demon arises—the demon of pride, the demon of being self-sufficient and not depending on anyone, the demon of judging those who are different from us—whatever our demon may be.

For many people, temptations are not urges to do evil, but can actually arise out of the goodness that we desire for ourselves alone. When we are able to follow the example of Jesus and take the time to reflect, not just to act on our temptations, we can turn them into occasions of goodness. For within each temptation is the challenge to discover the opposite side of the demon or the virtue or goodness that matches that vice or evil.

For example, if we are tempted by pride, we can reflect on the people who helped us develop our talents and pray for them and express our gratitude to God for the gift of our abilities. We can go further and examine how we can use these talents in service of others. If our demon is anger, we can reflect on how to turn that human response into upholding the convictions we have and energetically defending the rights of those who are poor. Perhaps we are tempted by the demon of inordinate worry, whereas, when we let go and have trust in God, we can live in the freedom and peacefulness that liberate us to use our energies in another positive direction.

As a community, we may give in to the temptation of silence in the face of injustice and neglect of the poor whom Jesus favours. The 'virtuous' side of this demon has many faces. When we gather our collective strength to bring about whatever change justice calls for, or when I alone recognise our communal neglect and challenge others to right relationship with those who are forgotten or ignored, we face the demon of our virtues.

Invitation to Group Sharing

1. What aspect in the story of Jesus in the desert is most striking to me?

2. Often demons are cleverly hidden. They may even appear to be virtues. What can help me recognise and name my demons when they tempt me?

3. How have my ideas of the devil and temptations changed or matured as I have grown in experience? What advice could I give to others about being patient in overcoming demons?

4. What might be temptations that our community or I face? What attempts can we make to overcome them and act on the opposite virtues?

Invitation to Act

Determine a specific action (individual or group) that flows from your sharing. This should be your primary consideration. When choosing an individual action, determine what you will do and share it with the group. When choosing a group action, determine who will take responsibility for different aspects of the action. The following are secondary suggestions:

1. Spend time each day in your own desert of quiet time to pray for insight. Reflect on the temptations that come to you most frequently. Discover what is the opposite virtue and action to that temptation. Decide how you will put that virtue into practice and act on your decision.

2. Look at one of the opposites of a demon you face. Ask a friend to help you take a step in that direction.

3. Decide what is a temptation to your community. What could be an action in opposition to that demon? Determine how you will take action as a group.

Invitation to Closing Prayer
Give thanks to God (aloud or silently) for insights gained, for desires awakened, for directions clarified, for the gift of one another's openness and sensitivity. Conclude with the following:

Loving Father of Jesus and our own Father,
lead us during this Lent through the desert we face each day.
We come with humility and openness
to recognise and name our temptations as Jesus did in the desert.
Send your Holy Spirit to help us in this task
and with the challenge we face
of walking the path of the opposite good.
These things we ask through Christ our Lord.
Amen

SECOND SUNDAY OF LENT

Faith and Spiritual Journey

Invitation to Pray
Pause for a few moments of silence and enter more deeply into the presence of God.

> ***Song:*** "At the Name of Jesus," Caroline Maria Noel

> ***Proclaim the gospel:*** Matthew 17:1-9
> The Transfiguration of Jesus

Take a few minutes to savour a word, a phrase, a question, or a feeling that rises up in you. Reflect on this quietly or share it aloud.

Invitation to Reflect
Jesus' face became as brilliant as the sun, his clothes, as shining as the light. Can you imagine how amazing this was for the apostles? Here they were given a glimpse of glory to strengthen their faith in Jesus for the journey ahead. Peter wanted to stay in this time and place that was heaven-like. Most of us do want to stay in the place where we feel safe and happy and comfortable, to hold on to the times of great joy, not to experience pain and difficulty. But Jesus says that is not the way it is to be. We must all walk the path of life that challenges us. We must each face the difficulties ahead, even continue to challenge ourselves with the gospel message in new ways.

We, too, will be transformed when we share in the Resurrection of Jesus. But that glory is already within us. For it does not come from the outside but the inside, like a seed planted within the earth waiting for us to nurture it. Each of us experiences moments of insight in our lives. Each of us will have times when we realise we are not doing all that God wants us to do. Each of us has that grace quietly waiting within us to do the courageous things, large and small, that the gospel message presents to us.

It is up to us, especially during Lent, to take the time to reflect so we can discover those voices that call us to a higher or deeper level of faith life. Lent is that journey in which we purify our desires of selfishness, when we walk up the mountain of Transfiguration with Jesus to hear his voice in our heart. Prayer, fasting, and almsgiving are the paths up that mountain, the traditional ways of purification. They are the windows through which we can look into ourselves and see where we can live more fully the life Jesus calls us to live. It is on the path of Lent, which reaches its fullness in Easter, that we can hear Jesus call us to repentance and a change of heart. It may be a call to be peacemakers, to love our enemies, to be the salt of the earth, to work to free those who are captives of prejudice or poverty, or to the many other actions in our power to transfigure the world around us.

Invitation to Group Sharing

1. Imagine being at the Transfiguration with Jesus and the apostles. What is it in this Scripture passage that especially speaks to me?

2. What in my past experiences of Lent has been helpful to me in hearing the gospel in a new way?

3. When have I had glimpses of insight or understanding that are like the light within me or the seed waiting to grow? What will I do to let my light shine before others or to sow seeds of understanding with others?

Invitation to Act

Determine a specific action (individual or group) that flows from your sharing. This should be your primary consideration. When choosing an individual action, determine what you will do and share it with the group. When choosing a group action, determine who will take responsibility for different aspects of the action. The following are secondary suggestions:

1. Name specific ways you will pray, fast, and give alms during this Lent. Share your plans with one friend.

2. Take time each day this week to talk to the Lord about ways you can grow the seed of faith you have been given.

3. Determine what "cause" you will, as a group, give alms to together at the end of Lent. Consider CAFOD, the Society of St. Vincent de Paul, or some local agency dealing with those in need.

Invitation to Closing Prayer
Give thanks to God (aloud or silently) for insights gained, for desires awakened, for directions clarified, for the gift of one another's openness and sensitivity. Conclude with the following:

Loving Father, we have put our hope in Jesus Christ
  who was transfigured before the apostles.
We believe that we, too, will share in that same glory.
Help us prepare for that time by our actions in this life.
Open our eyes to the seed within us waiting to grow
  and blossom into the good works that Jesus calls us to do.
Help us use this time of prayer, fasting, and almsgiving
  to come to a greater understanding
  and a determination to follow the call we have been given
  both as individuals and as a community.
This we ask in Jesus' name and in the power of the Holy Spirit.
Amen

THIRD SUNDAY OF LENT

Acceptance, Compassion, Dignity

Invitation to Pray
Pause for a few moments of silence and enter more deeply into the presence of God.

> *Song:* "Oh Living Water," Sr Virginia Vissing

> *Proclaim the gospel:* John 4:5-42
> The Samaritan Woman

Take a few minutes to savour a word, a phrase, a question, or a feeling that rises up in you. Reflect on this quietly or share it aloud.

Invitation to Reflect
In the meeting between Jesus and the Samaritan woman, we have a story with many levels of meaning. One of those comes late in the story when this woman, who started out speaking sarcastically in response to Jesus, ends up becoming an evangeliser. She leaves her water jar and the job she came to do and spreads the word about her conversation with Jesus, making many converts among those to whom she gives witness. Her own conversion of heart and mind, like that of so many of us, followed the path from surprise to sarcasm to interior belief.

The key in this whole episode is the way Jesus listened. He sat and patiently began a conversation with someone who disagreed with him, gently listening and responding, even breaking a religious law by talking with her and drinking from her jar. He did not lose patience when she was sarcastic and hostile. Being a woman and a Samaritan put her on the lowest rung of society. Being involved in public scandal made her even more of an outcast. Yet Jesus listened to her, talked with her in public, and offered her acceptance, compassion, and dignity.

Acceptance, compassion, and dignity— aren't these what each person desires? And how much more difficult that can be for those on the lower rungs of our society's ladder. In this story, Jesus shows us how we are to behave, tells us to whom we should reach out and listen.

In reaching out to this individual, Jesus, a Jew himself, reached out to so many in the Samaritan community: those who felt wronged by the Jews, those who felt discriminated against, and even those who were hostile to certain outsiders. One step, a conversation with one person, can have far-reaching effects. Who is it that you might have a conversation with, listening to his or her story, perhaps even to the hostility and sarcasm and quietly exchanging ideas? Who knows where such a meeting might lead? It may not change a whole society, but it can make a difference far beyond the two people who sit together like the man and woman who spoke to each other at the well.

Invitation to Group Sharing

1. In what ways do I identify with the Samaritan woman?

2. Who are the 'Samaritans' in our society? What fears do I have about talking with one of them or listening to his or her story as Jesus did?

3. How does our society as a whole sin against certain people or certain groups? How do I see my individual responsibility in this?

4. What can we, as a community, do to face these sins and change the status of certain groups?

Invitation to Act

Determine a specific action (individual or group) that flows from your sharing. This should be your primary consideration. When choosing an individual action, determine what you will do and share it with the group. When choosing a group action, determine who will take responsibility for different aspects of the action. The following are secondary suggestions:

1. In your own quiet, be in the presence of Jesus and listen to him as he did to the Samaritan woman, and hear what he tells you about the Samaritans in our midst—who they are, what he is calling you to do. Keep a journal on this reflection.

2. Name one social sin and brainstorm together five actions you could take to work against that specific sin.

3. In your parish, find out which groups are acting in compassionate ways and support their efforts.

4. Ask a family member, a friend, a co-worker, a neighbour, or a stranger how he or she is. Listen with your heart.

Invitation to Closing Prayer

Give thanks to God (aloud or silently) for insights gained, for desires awakened, for directions clarified, for the gift of one another's openness and sensitivity. Conclude with the following:

God, our wise and loving Father, in your wisdom you gave us the example of your Son who once again shows us the way to live the life you desire.

We ask you now for insight to see what his example in this story means for us in our own lives today.

We ask you for courage to do what Jesus did and to reach out to someone with patience, without judgment, and with the sensitivity needed to heal wounds and sinfulness of our time and our society.

We make our prayer through Jesus your Son and in the Holy Spirit. Amen

FOURTH SUNDAY OF LENT

New Hope of Dignity

Invitation to Pray
Pause for a few moments of silence and enter more deeply into the presence of God.

> *Song*: "Be Thou my Vision," 8th C Irish, Tr. Mary Byrne

> *Proclaim the gospel:* John 9:1-41
> The Man Born Blind

Take a few minutes to savour a word, a phrase, a question, or a feeling that rises up in you. Reflect on this quietly or share it aloud.

Invitation to Reflect
This long and powerful story is divided into several parts: the first is a theological discussion of the cause of the man's blindness. Here Jesus teaches that blindness is not due to sin and that God's glory will be seen through the blind man. Next we hear how the miracle took place with the mud and the washing of his eyes in the Pool of Siloam. Following this comes a description of the reactions to the miracle. The neighbours can hardly believe it is the same person; the man himself confesses who the person is who did this; some Pharisees accuse Jesus of healing on the Sabbath, and try to bring the man's parents into the discussion and challenge the man himself. Upon his confession of faith, he is thrown out of the synagogue. Jesus finds him again and has his final exchange of words with some of the Pharisees.

Jesus went out to the blind man. Although there was a crowd around because of the feast days going on, this one individual was important enough that Jesus would take time to do whatever he could to help. He not only cured him of his physical condition, but Jesus gave him new hope and a purpose in life—faith in Jesus as sent from God. The man became a disciple through faith and through Jesus' reaching out to him as an individual. Each person, Jesus shows us, is worthy of dignity no matter who he or she is. Our own lack of sight can keep us from recognizing someone's dignity.

Like the people who challenged Jesus' actions and the man's belief, we, too, can choose to stay in our blindness or we can choose to receive the gift of sight. But to be able to see the beauty, the value of each person, we must first recognise and admit our own blindness. Unlike Jesus, we can be tempted to stay in our safe harbour, keeping with individuals who are similar to us. There we all think the same, look the same, disapprove of the same things and people. Such blindness and fear can keep us from recognising, as Jesus did, the value of each individual, regardless of who or what he or she is. Perhaps we are jealous because of what the person has or who he or she is. Or perhaps we refuse hospitality and openness to someone because of what we have and who we think we are. In either case, we may miss the great opportunity to overcome our own blindness and see the Jesus who is there, waiting to offer us sight and new eyes of faith.

Invitation to Group Sharing

1. With whom in this story does my heart empathise? The parents who were afraid of being excluded from the community? The blind man? Those who thought the law was the most important thing to follow instead of the human need for which Jesus seemed to break the laws?

2. Describe a situation where blindness may have kept you or someone else from missing an opportunity to connect with others. What enabled me to overcome such blindness? How did I feel afterward? What did I learn from this experience?

3. Share about a time when Jesus sought you out and healed you.

4. How do I see our community reaching out to individuals who may be on the edge of life? How could we improve in this regard?

Invitation to Act

Determine a specific action (individual or group) that flows from your sharing. This should be your primary consideration. When choosing an individual action, determine what you will do and share it with the group. When choosing a group action, determine who will take responsibility for different aspects of the action. The following are secondary suggestions:

1. During this week, offer hospitality of some kind to one person with whom you wouldn't ordinarily relate. Perhaps share a cup of coffee or take a walk together.

2. Set aside time this week to think about your own blindness and

where it might occur. Pray to be aware of this blindness in a special way during Lent so you can be open to the gift of sight that is offered. Perhaps copy a passage from this gospel on an index card. Keep the card handy so you can reflect on the verse several times a day. Jot down any inspirations or share a resolution with a friend.

3. Discuss who may feel like outsiders in your parish community. Decide together on one action you can take to help your parish be more welcoming to such individuals.

Invitation to Closing Prayer
Give thanks to God (aloud or silently) for insights gained, for desires awakened, for directions clarified, for the gift of one another's openness and sensitivity. Conclude with the following:

Father of mercy and kindness, your loving Son Jesus
    responded with his heart to an individual outside of the
    mainstream.
He led the blind man into the community, giving both to him
    and the community new eyes, new vision, new hope.
We praise and thank you for this marvelous lesson and
    ask your help as we try to follow in Jesus' footsteps.
Help us to discover our own blindness and to rejoice in the new
    vision we receive when we act to overcome that blindness.
We ask this through Christ our Lord and in the Holy Spirit.
Amen

FIFTH SUNDAY OF LENT

Raising From the Dead

Invitation to Pray
Pause for a few moments of silence and enter more deeply into the presence of God.

> *Song:* "I am the Bread of Life," (verses 1, 4 and 5) Suzanne Toolan

> *Proclaim the gospel:* John 11:1-45
> The Raising of Lazarus

Take a few minutes to savour a word, a phrase, a question, or a feeling that rises up in you. Reflect on this quietly or share it aloud.

Invitation to Reflect
This emotional and dramatic story is Jesus' last miracle and sign before his own Passion and Death. In a way, the death and resurrection of Jesus' friend, Lazarus, points the way to the Death and Resurrection of Jesus. Both of them show that Jesus is the true Messiah but Lazarus was raised from the dead for a brief time. Jesus was raised forever. Jesus made eternal life possible for all of us through the gift of his life. Before raising Lazarus, Jesus prayed to the Father. This was not so much a prayer of petition, but a prayer revealing his own close relationship with the Father. As a result of this miracle, two things happened: some believed in him because of what they had seen; others conspired to have him executed because he was a threat.

This reading is about the resurrection of Lazarus, the Resurrection of Jesus, and our own resurrection. The Scripture scholar, Carroll Stuhlmueller, reminds us that the resurrection is a religious experience, not a theological problem to be solved. It is not a miracle happening outside of us, but is the transforming power of Jesus within us. It is complete only when we invite and accept the Spirit of Jesus to dwell within us individually, and within all of us as the same family of God. When this happens, we live life in a new way. It is as if we put on new glasses to see the world around us through his eyes, not ours. It changes the way we view people, events, and the things that happen in our own lives. It causes us to act differently and even do things we never thought we had the courage to do.

The disciples, as well as the family and friends of Lazarus, felt hopeless when Jesus didn't arrive in time to prevent the death of Lazarus. Hopeless is not a word that has meaning for those of us who believe in the resurrection that Jesus proclaimed here. Jesus embraced hopelessness and became hope for the world. Thus, fear loses its control over those who believe in the Resurrection—his and ours. Just as Jesus took away the stone from the tomb of Lazarus, he takes away the stone of despair in our lives. Our own disappointments, failures, frustrations, and losses contain the seed of hope and new life, for they are passing. The Resurrection shows us that life itself is eternal.

Invitation to Group Sharing

1. What is the most striking or significant word, phrase, or feeling in this gospel reading?

2. Lazarus was bound by the wrappings of funeral cloth. What are some ways I am still bound and need to be set free? What are some wrappings I have been given? What are some wrappings I have put on myself?

3. In what specific ways do I overcome the everyday despair and hopelessness the world offers? Participate in the Mass? Spend time with Scripture? Listen to my favourite musical artist? Take a walk? Are there some less uplifting methods I use to deaden my pain, for example, grabbing a cigarette, reaching for a drink or a drug, picking away at a tub of ice cream?

4. How does having hope affect the way our life is lived? Give an example from your own life, if possible. What can I or we, as a group, do to help instill hope in someone who feels hopeless?

Invitation to Act

Determine a specific action (individual or group) that flows from your sharing. This should be your primary consideration. When choosing an individual action, determine what you will do and share it with the group. When choosing a group action, determine who will take responsibility for different aspects of the action. The following are secondary suggestions:

1. Pray this week for the light to see where you are bound and need

to be set free from fears, prejudices, areas of conflict, habits, limitations or sins from which Jesus is calling you to arise. Take one step toward loosing a bond that keeps you from living as a resurrected person.

2. Spend time this week with someone who is in need of hope or of time with an uplifting person. Bring to him or her the joy that you, as a follower of Christ, experience.

3. Join with this group or others in an action to unbind the cloths that keep the community from being the open and accepting family Christ desires us to be.

Invitation to Closing Prayer
Give thanks to God (aloud or silently) for insights gained, for desires awakened, for directions clarified, for the gift of one another's openness and sensitivity. Conclude with the following:

Good and gracious Father,
when your Son Jesus raised Lazarus from the dead,
he showed that we will be given new life.
We walk every day in the light and hope of resurrection.
Help us to live each day in gratitude for the gift of our very being.
Move our hearts and minds to share the gifts of life and hope.
Help us to seek freedom from all the bonds that still hold us.
Help us to reach out to those outside our community's acceptance.
We remember especially_____(name silently or aloud.)
We pray this through Christ our Lord and in the unity of the
Holy Spirit.
Amen

PALM SUNDAY

Suffering with Integrity

Invitation to Pray
Pause for a few moments of silence and enter more deeply into the presence of God.

> *Song:* "All Glory, Laud, and Honour," Theodulph of Orleans, Tr. by John M. Neale

> *Proclaim the gospel:* Matthew 26:14—27:66
> The Passion

Take a few minutes to savour a word, a phrase, a question, or a feeling that rises up in you. Reflect on this quietly or share it aloud.

Invitation to Reflect
Each year on this Sunday we read a different Bible account of the Passion of Jesus. In Cycle C we read the story from the Gospel of Luke, in Cycle B from Mark and this year, in Cycle A, we read it from the Gospel according to Matthew. Every Good Friday, the Gospel of John is read. There are differences among these accounts, as the observant listener knows. The version we have just heard introduces popular stories about the dream of Pilate's wife as well as instructional material from the Old Testament. These varying perspectives bless us with different viewpoints and emphases that can speak to us in many ways. They also enrich our experience of trying to enter into the experience of Jesus during these days.

Regardless of which gospel we hear, we must listen with our hearts. Professor James Fowler, author of various books, including *Stages of Faith: The Psychology of Human Development and the Quest for Meaning,* describes that experience as "Rather than reading the word, I let the word read me." It is in the heart that we can meet the suffering Jesus, the fearful disciples, the concerned wife of Pilate and all the others who participated in this drama. This is how we can know deeply the importance of this story, which may be so familiar that its drama and greatness and gruesomeness pass over us too lightly.

It is the suffering Messiah whom we meet in this drama. Although the suffering we experience in no way compares with that of Jesus, it is in suffering that we can meet on common ground. Each person suffers in his or her own way. Some suffer physical hardship and pain. Others have interior suffering of loneliness or emotional or mental illness, or of helplessly watching loved ones in pain. When we open our eyes and our hearts, we see suffering all around us in the world. There are hungry children; people living in streets; elderly who are lonely; men, women, and children who are innocent victims of cruel wars. The end of Jesus' life shows us how to face our own suffering. Jesus is our model, for he lived his life and faced his terrible suffering with integrity and obedience. The whole of Jesus' life shows us how to face the suffering of others. In his public life, he did all he could to overcome the evil and suffering he met. Ultimately, his own suffering and death give us the chance to live in happiness, peace, joy, and a life forever free of suffering in the future.

Invitation to Group Sharing

1. James Fowler describes his experience as, "Rather than reading the word, I let the word read me." How will I allow the Word to read, move, or form me?

2. What image in this long gospel passage stays in my mind? How does the word or image read me?

3. Think of the various 'players' in this Passion drama: Peter, Judas, Pilate and the others. In what way can I identify with them?

4. What lesson does Jesus' suffering teach me about my own suffering? How can this lesson help me feel the suffering of those in distant lands or those removed from my everyday life?

5. What is the suffering that most calls to me to reach out in some way? How will I do that?

Invitation to Act

Determine a specific action (individual or group) that flows from your sharing. This should be your primary consideration. When choosing an individual action, determine what you will do and share it with the group. When choosing a group action, determine who will take responsibility for different aspects of the action. The following are secondary suggestions:

1. As a group, choose one person or one group whose suffering you can take a step to ease. Decide how and when you will take an action needed.

2. Find out from your parish or diocese which groups are involved in working to eliminate some kind of suffering, visiting the sick, feeding the hungry, helping the homeless. Offer to make yourself available to them.

3. Spend time each day this week thinking about the suffering of Jesus and looking for his face in the suffering you see around you and read or hear about on the news. Pray for the persons in each story.

4. Determine who in your parish or community suffers in silence— divorced or single parents, those persons living with HIV/AIDS, the elderly, or others. Join or develop an outreach ministry to help ease their pain. Consider inviting them to form a small Christian community.

Invitation to Closing Prayer
Give thanks to God (aloud or silently) for insights gained, for desires awakened, for directions clarified, for the gift of one another's openness and sensitivity. Conclude with the following:

Alone we can do nothing, O Father.
You sent your Son Jesus, who suffered greatly so that we would never be alone.
Help us in our own suffering to be one with him, to lean on his strength and believe with hopeful hearts.
Be with us in the steps we take this week and in the future to do something to lessen the suffering of another of your beloved children, our brothers and sisters.
These things we ask through Christ our Lord.
Amen

Easter Season

EASTER SUNDAY

Amazing Good News

Invitation to Pray
Pause for a few moments of silence and enter more deeply into the presence of God.

> ***Song***: "Jesus Christ is Risen Today," Lyra Davidica
> ***Proclaim the gospel:*** John 20:1-9
> The Empty Tomb

Take a few minutes to savour a word, a phrase, a question, or a feeling that rises up in you. Reflect on this quietly or share it aloud.

Invitation to Reflect
Look again at the ending of this reading: "For they did not yet understand the Scripture that he had to rise from the dead" (v. 9). Sometimes we lose that statement when we hear this gospel passage. The disciples at the tomb were confused, they were disbelieving, they were afraid, astonished, thought his body had been stolen, and perhaps had even more reactions. We know for sure they didn't understand what had happened. Their discovery of the empty tomb really did not make sense until Jesus later began to appear to his friends.

In a way, the good news they discovered was too good to be true. Sometimes it also takes us a long time to let any wonderful, amazing, good news seep into our hearts and minds. No wonder the disciples were slow to believe. Yet, Easter is the keystone of the whole life of Jesus. Without Easter, his life, which had promised so very much would have been, if not a failure, a huge disappointment. However, because of the Resurrection, everything in his ministry has an amazing significance. Because of the Resurrection, his disciples, including the doubters who visited the tomb that first Easter, began the mission of the Church. That mission continues today in the life of the Church, in our own hearts and words and actions.

Invitation to Group Sharing
1. With which one of the followers in this story do I most identify: Mary, who ran to tell others about the confusing scene and perhaps thought the body had been stolen; the first disciple, who

61

only looked in the tomb and believed that Jesus had risen; Peter, who had to go in and examine things? Why? What might this tell me about myself?

2. I am here today because I believe in the Resurrection. What makes it believable to me? Do I find it as astonishing as the disciples did? How important is it to me that Jesus did rise from the dead?

3. What experiences of death/resurrection have I had in my own life and what have I learned from them?

4. How does the Resurrection give me hope or influence my life? What positive action can I take to share this with one who needs hope?

Invitation to Act
Determine a specific action (individual or group) that flows from your sharing. This should be your primary consideration. When choosing an individual action, determine what you will do and share it with the group. When choosing a group action, determine who will take responsibility for different aspects of the action. The following are secondary suggestions:

1. Continue celebrating and observing this most important liturgical season during the coming weeks and not just during the days close to the feast. Decide how you can continue celebrating the Resurrection in this season.

2. Share your hope and belief in resurrection with someone who has experienced a recent death and who may not be able to see good news in his or her life just now.

3. Decide what your group might do to welcome those just initiated into your community through the Rite of Christian Initiation of Adults (RCIA) process so that they are integrated into the parish community and not abandoned after Easter.

Invitation to Closing Prayer
Give thanks to God (aloud or silently) for insights gained, for desires awakened, for directions clarified, for the gift of one another's openness and sensitivity. Conclude with the following:

This wonderful day, O Christ, is yours.
Help us to experience Easter in our hearts.
Turn our own empty tombs into signs of new life, signs of hope.
Give us the grace to share our hope with those we love
and especially with those who need new life
and courage and hope in their own lives.

Alleluia, Amen

SECOND SUNDAY OF EASTER

Becoming Peacemakers

Invitation to Pray
Pause for a few moments of silence and enter more deeply into the presence of God.

> *Song:* "The Strife is O'er," Tr. by Francis Pott

> *Proclaim the gospel:* John 20:19-31
> Appearance to the Disciples

Take a few minutes to savour a word, a phrase, a question, or a feeling that rises up in you. Reflect on this quietly or share it aloud.

Invitation to Reflect
Peace is the first thing Jesus offers the disciples after the Resurrection. After that, he offers them the Holy Spirit. Finally, he asks them to be forgivers, people who do not hold grudges, who do not build walls between people, but to be people who are unifiers.

To the disciples, Jesus' greeting of peace is important and symbolic. The Jews, the people of Israel, always knew that a reign of peace would come when the Messiah came, and this would mean that people would live in harmony with one other. In this reading, we notice that Jesus emphasised this coming of peace by offering it to them not once, but twice. This would underline its importance to Jesus and to the disciples, for it showed that the reign of God was at hand.

As Paul and Luke show us, the greatest disgraces in the early Christian community were disharmony and lack of peace. Remember how people were converted by watching the believers and saying you could tell they were Christians by seeing how they loved one another. This unity and overcoming of differences and disagreements could be a powerful sign to people today, as well. The message Jesus gave the disciples is as relevant now as it was then. We are to be peacemakers, to forgive those who offend us, for this will bring about unity and will do away with discord.

When Jesus breathed on the disciples and gave them the Holy Spirit, he was offering the Spirit so that they could accomplish that same peace and harmony among themselves, among God's people. It is this Spirit who would help them create peace in the community and would also be with them as they went to heal the sick, forgive sins, and proclaim that Jesus, the Messiah, had come. It is this Spirit who is with us as we travel the roads of our own lives.

"Blessed are those who have not seen and yet believe" (v. 29). Jesus is talking to us who see him not in a locked room, but where he lives and walks and talks in our own community, in the people in our parish, in our town, in our family, in our workplace, and in people across the world. Jesus is there for those who have eyes of faith.

Invitation to Group Sharing

1. Recall a time you experienced the peace or forgiveness that Jesus models. What was it like before and after this event? What can I learn from this experience?

2. What similarities can I find between the early Christian community and the one in which I live? What does this say to me about the gift of faith?

3. A time I believe the Holy Spirit was present in a situation in my life or in someone else's life was_____.

4. When do I find myself like Thomas? When have I been like those who have not seen? What will I do to encourage another who does not believe?

Invitation to Act

Determine a specific action (individual or group) that flows from your sharing. This should be your primary consideration. When choosing an individual action, determine what you will do and share it with the group. When choosing a group action, determine who will take responsibility for different aspects of the action. The following are secondary suggestions:

1. Spend time prayerfully examining a conflict in which you are currently involved. Listen to what the Holy Spirit may lead you to understand and to do. Ask someone to help you take that action, if necessary.

2. Name a way in which your town or city is not responding to needs as well as it could. Become involved in a group, commit-

tee or organisation that is trying to build up the community in a positive way.

3.   As a group, take an action for those who are poor, elderly, or for others without a voice in the community.

Invitation to Closing Prayer

Give thanks to God (aloud or silently) for insights gained, for desires awakened, for directions clarified, for the gift of one another's openness and sensitivity. Conclude with the following:

Heavenly Father, we thank you for the words, example, and actions of your Son Jesus, which give us the path to follow.
We are grateful for the Spirit who comes to be with us on our journey on the path of unity, of forgiveness, of care, and of love for one another.
Help us to be witnesses to others of a community of baptised believers, graced with the Resurrection of Jesus and the presence of the Spirit.

Alleluia, Amen

THIRD SUNDAY OF EASTER

Eyes of Faith

Invitation to Pray
Pause for a few moments of silence and enter more deeply into the presence of God.

> *Song:* "I Will Be With You," Gerald Markland
> *Proclaim the gospel:* Luke 24:13-35
> The Appearance on the Road to Emmaus

Take a few minutes to savour a word, a phrase, a question, or a feeling that rises up in you. Reflect on this quietly or share it aloud.

Invitation to Reflect
The story of the two disciples on the road to Emmaus is an important one for each of us trying to find Jesus in our lives. We can identify with the disciples in this story. Jesus was with them in every step they took—and they did not recognise him. The same is true for us. Jesus is with us in every step we take, in every breath we breathe, in every word we speak. But our eyes are not always opened, our hearts do not always burn with recognising him or with admitting to ourselves that he is here.

For the disciples, physically seeing Jesus was not enough. They needed to understand the Word of God and believe with eyes of faith. So blind were they that they tried to teach Jesus about their friend Jesus and what had happened in Jerusalem. In truth, they were the ones who did not understand or see clearly. They were in pain and crushed with disappointment. They thought their Saviour had been a failure.

The disciples in the story can seem amazing to us. But then, how can we ourselves not see that he is with us? We believe he is present, and we have the Scriptures and the Eucharist where we can meet him. All we need to do is say his name. We have a community, the Church, to call upon to confirm our belief and be his presence to us. But especially when we are in pain or feeling depressed or experiencing disappointment, it can be as hard for us as for the disciples to see and believe that Jesus is truly with us. Jesus would never abandon us any more than he would the disciples, for he is the Good Shepherd who does not abandon his flock. We see his death and Resurrection, and as we experience whatever kind of death we are feeling, we know that the resurrection does follow. We know this as clearly as the disciples did after their eyes were opened. Experience shows us that in the midst of death, it can be hardest to believe, or else it can be that the belief, the knowledge, the faith are precisely what bring us through to the resurrection.

Invitation to Group Sharing

1. When have I been depressed and disappointed like the disciples on the road? When am I like them after they recognised Jesus? What role did my faith play in that experience?

2. A time in my life when I had a moment of enlightenment, when my heart burned, when a light went on for me, and I saw things in a new or clearer way was _____. What did I learn from this?

3. When am I called upon to be as Jesus was with the disciples? To listen to someone who is suffering emotionally or physically? To invite someone to share our hospitality? To pray for another? To be Jesus' presence in someone's time of need? What will I do to be present to another?

Invitation to Act

Determine a specific action (individual or group) that flows from your sharing. This should be your primary consideration. When choosing an individual action, determine what you will do and share it with the group. When choosing a group action, determine who will take responsibility for different aspects of the action. The following are secondary suggestions:

1. The disciples saw Jesus more clearly when they listened again to the Scriptures they had heard many times before and when they broke bread with Jesus. Take fifteen minutes each day to visit the Scriptures again. Try to understand Jesus and his message in a new way that is helpful to your life.

2. Name someone who may need your attentive presence or your comforting hospitality. Make plans to be with that person.

3. As a group, make plans to join together for a meal and decide whom else you might invite. Read the Scriptures and share your thoughts before eating together.

Invitation to Closing Prayer

Give thanks to God (aloud or silently) for insights gained, for desires awakened, for directions clarified, for the gift of one another's openness and sensitivity. Conclude with the following:

Father in heaven,
you sent Jesus to die and rise,
to teach and feed us.
Just as he was present to the disciples of Emmaus
and their eyes were opened,
help us to recognise him this day and each day
as he walks with us.
Help us to follow his example
and to listen with care and compassion to those in pain.
Give us the wisdom to respond as he would in our place.
We ask this through Jesus and in the Holy Spirit.
Amen

FOURTH SUNDAY OF EASTER

"I am the Gate of the Sheepfold."

Invitation to Pray
Pause for a few moments of silence and enter more deeply into the presence of God.

> *Song:* "The Lord's my Shepherd," from the Scottish Psalter

> *Proclaim the gospel:* John 10:1-10
>   The Good Shepherd

Take a few minutes to savour a word, a phrase, a question, or a feeling that rises up in you. Reflect on this quietly or share it aloud.

Invitation to Reflect
In the time of Jesus, at the end of each day, when their sheep were finished grazing, all the shepherds would bring their flocks together for the night. They would keep them safely in a protected fold so that wolves or thieves would not bother them. Every night one shepherd was appointed to lie down in front of the gate of the sheepfold so that no one could enter. This shepherd would protect the flocks even with his life, if necessary. Each morning all the shepherds would return and call or whistle for their own sheep to gather. Each knew his own sheep and the sheep knew the sound of their shepherd's voice and would follow him.

The Good Shepherd is not the shepherd of pious art, but a strong and brave protector who lies down in front of the gate refusing to let anyone snatch us or come near us. The Good Shepherd, Jesus, knows each of us by name and calls us in baptism. When life experiences such as family crises, death, illness, fear, or emotional pain make us unable to move or unable to care for ourselves, he is there to guard us, to protect us, and to lead us through the darkest hours. Sometimes it is only long after the event that we recognise he was there, is there for us. Taking time to recall those experiences helps us be aware of them the next time and take comfort and courage from his presence.

The Good Shepherd is also an example for us to learn who and how we are to be for one other. The Good Shepherd is the pattern for us to model our lives. We are to go out of our way to protect and care for others. We are to

70

watch over those who need watching over. Indeed, we are to search for them, not just wait for our paths to cross. In our own community, there are those who are forgotten, helpless, and those who are in some way lost. Jesus calls us to be shepherds to them. Jesus has been the Good Shepherd for us individually and for our community. How can we not do the same for others?

Invitation to Group Sharing

1. In what ways have I experienced Jesus, the Good Shepherd?

2. Who are the thieves and wolves that prey on the helpless or vulnerable in our midst?

3. How can our parish and I welcome the sheep who need protecting and calling by name? What can I or we do to make them feel more welcome? What resources can we use? How creative can we be?

Invitation to Act

Determine a specific action (individual or group) that flows from your sharing. This should be your primary consideration. When choosing an individual action, determine what you will do and share it with the group. When choosing a group action, determine who will take responsibility for different aspects of the action. The following are secondary suggestions:

1. Reach out to someone who may be a silent person in need, for example, invite someone who lives alone to sit with you in church; have coffee with someone who recently lost a family member; ask your school head teacher if there is a child who needs a friend to read a story.

2. Join with others in the parish or the larger community who have found a way to be protectors, guardians, or advocates for the vulnerable.

3. As a group and without breaking confidences, commit yourselves to a week of prayer for someone in need.

4. Recall times in your life when you were in a crisis. Pray in thanksgiving for anyone who was like a Good Shepherd to you.

Invitation to Closing Prayer
Give thanks to God (aloud or silently) for insights gained, for desires awakened, for directions clarified, for the gift of one another's openness and sensitivity. Conclude with the following:

Loving Father,
with grateful hearts we acknowledge the gift of your Son,
our Shepherd.
Help us learn to recognise his voice
when it is spoken to us every day,
but especially when we are vulnerable
and need protection and strength.
Give us the heart of a Good Shepherd, that we, too,
will care for those who are vulnerable, anxious, lonely.
Help us to recognise ourselves in them
and to reach out to them in times of need.
We pray in union with the Holy Spirit, through Christ our Lord.
Amen

FIFTH SUNDAY OF EASTER

"Do Not Let Your Hearts Be Troubled."

Invitation to Pray
Pause for a few moments of silence and enter more deeply into the presence of God.

> ***Song:*** "Be Not Afraid," Robert J. Dufford, SJ

> ***Proclaim the gospel:*** John 14:1-12
> Last Supper Discourse

Take a few minutes to savour a word, a phrase, a question, or a feeling that rises up in you. Reflect on this quietly or share it aloud.

Invitation to Reflect
"Do not let your hearts be troubled. You have faith in God; have faith also in me" (v. 1). This invitation of Jesus to the apostles is the same invitation he gives to each of us. Yet, our hearts are troubled. Why? For Thomas it was the desire, the need to have clarity about what lay ahead for him, for all of them. What was the path like? Where was it going? Where was Jesus going?

For Philip it seems also to be a question of being in control. "Master, show us the Father, and that will be enough for us" (v. 8). "Just give us certainty, clarity, control and we'll believe," he says. "That's all we ask!"

Looking back from where we stand in history, both of their responses might seem outrageous. Jesus, after all, is God, our Saviour, and he was going home to his Father in heaven to prepare a place for his disciples. But how different are we, really, from these troubled disciples? Do we not hold on to controlling our lives? How often we even fool ourselves into believing that we *are* in charge, in control. Sometimes our own hearts are troubled about the future, about what is going to become of us tomorrow.

This gospel message is one of hope and of how much we are cared for and loved. Jesus seems to understand what a difficult message it is for us to believe. For he says that if they cannot believe his words, look at his actions, the works he has done. Jesus says to us exactly what he said to Thomas and Philip: "Do not let your hearts be troubled" (v. 1). That invitation, that commandment could be our daily meditation for the rest of our lives: "Do not let your hearts be troubled".

Invitation to Group Sharing

1. What is my response to this gospel?

2. A time when my heart was troubled was _____. The way I dealt with it was _____.

3. In what ways can I relate to Thomas and to Philip?

4. Jesus said we know the way to where he is going because we know him. We do not walk this path alone, but we walk it as a community, a people with our God. How has my faith community been helpful in showing me the path and helping me stay on it? How can I or we do this for others?

Invitation to Act

Determine a specific action (individual or group) that flows from your sharing. This should be your primary consideration. When choosing an individual action, determine what you will do and share it with the group. When choosing a group action, determine who will take responsibility for different aspects of the action. The following are secondary suggestions:

1. Meditate on Jesus' words: "Do not let your hearts be troubled" (v. 1). What causes your heart to be troubled? Pray for the help you need to listen and obey Jesus' words.

2. Invite a friend or friends to share stories of the paths of their lives. What have been the main stopping points on that path? When were you least in control and what happened when you realised that? What wisdom can you share from your experience?

3. Discover through the news this week a troubled person, a group of people or a country. Is there anything you can to to alleviate fear.

4. Celebrate the Eucharist with a group this week and rejoice in Jesus' presence. Perhaps have a meal together afterward. Share the message of hope and trust in Jesus' care with someone who feels lonely or abandoned.

Invitation to Closing Prayer

Give thanks to God (aloud or silently) for insights gained, for desires awakened, for directions clarified, for the gift of one another's openness and sensitivity. Conclude with the following:

Use Psalm 33 from Sunday's liturgy or the prayer below.

Loving Father,
the earth is full of your kindness,
which is in every step we take along the path
to the home you share with your Son Jesus.
Open our eyes to see our many blessings.
Open our hearts to have confidence
in your promise and faith in the words of Jesus.
Free us from trying to create our own paths
and help us to follow the path you have placed before us.
Then our hearts will not be troubled,
but will be filled with joyful peace.
These things we pray in confidence through Christ our Lord.
Amen

Sixth Sunday of Easter

Hope: The Paraclete Abides with Us

Invitation to Pray
Pause for a few moments of silence and enter more deeply into the presence of God.

> *Song:* "This Is My Body," Jimmy Owens & Damian Lundy

> *Proclaim the gospel:* John 14:15-21
> The Spirit of Truth Remains with Us

Take a few minutes to savour a word, a phrase, a question, or a feeling that rises up in you. Reflect on this quietly or share it aloud.

Invitation to Reflect
There is, perhaps, no greater assurance in times of trouble than the promise, "I'll be there with you," from someone we trust. We may have heard that from a parent when we were small children afraid of the dark. Perhaps our best friend said it when we were teenagers craving acceptance, or our spouse slipped it in when we were newly married and seeking the job of our dreams. Or it could have been said during a troubled pregnancy or, and this is one of the most painful of all, when we lost a loved one through death or divorce.

Jesus himself knew the need for reassurance in times of trouble. He had the need as a human and could offer it as the God among us. In Sunday's gospel passage, he extends those words to his closest companions who had literally 'walked the walk' with him on many a missionary journey, sharing in his healing and teaching ministry. Jesus knows they are about to experience his transition from daily mentor and teacher to resurrected Lord. And he knows what they will need to become the Church that continues the mission. So he promises nothing less than his own Spirit to come as Advocate. The Divine Friend will not come and go, but will abide, reside, and stay as Jesus' followers live and minister in his name.

This Gospel is *very good news* for us. We are told the precious secret that will make the difference between orphan existence and full life in a believing and serving community. All the while, the Advocate will accompany the community, assisting us to seek the just and true and challenge all that brings death. In this way, we, the Church, are encouraged for mission. He will 'be there for us' now and always.

Invitation to Group Sharing

1. In my life experience, when has the Spirit been an advocate for me in times of trouble? In what ways did hope return to me?

2. Is my awareness of God's helpful presence becoming clearer, deeper, more frequent? How does this affect my day?

3. What groups in our parish, neighborhood, or society seem most abandoned in time of trouble? Who are today's 'orphaned'?

4. What is one concrete and practical step we can take this week to reach a contemporary 'orphan' who needs to hear, "I am there with you"?

Invitation to Act

Determine a specific action (individual or group) that flows from your sharing. This should be your primary consideration. When choosing an individual action, determine what you will do and share it with the group. When choosing a group action, determine who will take responsibility for different aspects of the action. The following are secondary suggestions:

1. Phone a relative or friend who shared a concern or problem with you recently. Ask how things are going now, and offer the reassuring words, "I am with you." (Pray before the call that he or she feels the presence of the Advocate through your contact.)

2. Try to be especially sensitive when you hear an individual express feelings of being orphaned or abandoned. This could be a parent about to see a child go off to university or marry. Be an inclusive, loving presence.

3. Affirm a child or spouse who has felt put down by you in the past. This may be all the assurance he or she needs to believe in himself or herself again!

Invitation to Closing Prayer

Give thanks to God (aloud or silently) for insights gained, for desires awakened, for directions clarified, for the gift of one another's openness and sensitivity. Conclude with the following:

Side 1:   Ever-present God,
          we are grateful that
          your Holy Spirit never leaves us.

Side 2:   Help us become people
          whose words and actions
          reassure those who feel orphaned.

All: Guide us to choose what is true and good,
          and thus continue your mission in our world.

          In Jesus' name we pray.
          Amen

SEVENTH SUNDAY OF EASTER

Jesus' Mission - and Ours

Invitation to Pray
Pause for a few moments of silence and enter more deeply into the presence of God.

> ***Song:*** "Alleluia, Sing to Jesus," W Chatterton Dix

> ***Proclaim the gospel:*** John 17:1-11a
> Jesus Accomplishes His Mission - and
> Ours Begins

Take a few minutes to savour a word, a phrase, a question, or a feeling that rises up in you. Reflect on this quietly or share it aloud.

Invitation to Reflect
"I remember a relative commenting at my mother's funeral that I resembled her. She said that it was in my look, talk, and laugh. I was both delighted and challenged to hear this. I had always admired my mother, but wondered if I could keep bringing her best qualities into my life."

Jesus would know what this speaker was feeling. His had been a clear-cut mission: to show people what God was like. To be the best face, the very Word of God, with his human face. Because Jesus was Son of God and second Person of the Trinity, he possessed God's nature and identity. Their communion was perfect and thoroughly intimate. That was why Jesus could be a credible face for God and an authentic witness to what God desired for people of Jesus' time. Through him, people would be able to know how loving God was.

For our speaker it had seemed natural for her to carry her mother's spirit in the future. It is sometimes harder for disciples of Jesus to imagine being entrusted with continuing his mission. Yet, we are promised all we need in today's gospel. Jesus tells God we know him because we believe in his revealed Word.

Jesus prayed to God that we and all future followers of his would be as faithful as he was in reflecting God who is love. With that kind of support, we may still struggle, but we have a grand and worthy mission.

Invitation to Group Sharing

1. Have I ever been compared to a person I considered good or holy? How did I feel? Were there lasting effects from the perceived resemblance?

2. When have I sensed I share in Jesus' mission to be the face of God? At home? In my workplace? In my ministry?

3. Does our parish or family have heroes whose qualities we want to share? Have we told them? Is Jesus one of these?

4. Are there some in our parish who have been hurt by a disciple of Jesus whose behaviour lacked justice or compassion? How can our prayer and ministry heal their disillusionment? What will we do to heal the hurt?

Invitation to Act

Determine a specific action (individual or group) that flows from your sharing. This should be your primary consideration. When choosing an individual action, determine what you will do and share it with the group. When choosing a group action, determine who will take responsibility for different aspects of the action. The following are secondary suggestions:

1. Review the means your parish provides to keep its members (today's disciples) equipped for continuing Jesus' mission. If there is a need to strengthen one component, such as Bible study, faith sharing in small communities, ministry training, or spiritual direction, act on this.

2. If you are a minister of hospitality at Mass or someone who serves refreshemnts after Mass, you are the face of God to strangers. Evaluate how well you resemble Jesus as you serve. Share your thoughts with another.

3. Participate in one activity that will help you better perform Jesus' ministry, for example, leisure, a lecture, reading, a movie.

4. Bring the needs of your loved ones to God in prayer.

Invitation to Closing Prayer
Give thanks to God (aloud or silently) for insights gained, for desires awakened, for directions clarified, for the gift of one another's openness and sensitivity. Conclude with the following:

Pray this litany of thanks together.

Leader: Because Jesus faithfully completed his mission, we say,

All: Praise and glory to you, O God!

Leader: Because Jesus has made God's love known to us, we say,

All: Praise and honour to you, O God!

Leader: Because we are entrusted with Jesus' mission today, we say,

All: Praise and thanks to you, O God!

PENTECOST SUNDAY

The Spirit's Gifts to All

Invitation to Pray
Pause for a few moments of silence and enter more deeply into the presence of God.

> *Song:* "Come Down, O Love Divine," Bianco da Siena, Tr. R F Littledale

> *Proclaim the gospel:* John 20:19-23
> The Disciples Receive the Spirit

Take a few minutes to savour a word, a phrase, a question, or a feeling that rises up in you. Reflect on this quietly or share it aloud.

Invitation to Reflect
Rabbi Abraham Heschel wrote in his spiritual journals a thought that became a conviction for him: "What we *own*, we *owe*." In the gospel reading, we hear Jesus confer a potent gift on the disciples: PEACE. First it is a greeting. Later, it becomes a mandate.

Offering peace seems an unlikely challenge for these followers, considering their circumstances. They are, at the moment, hiding behind locked doors, quaking from fear of the authorities. But true to his nature, the risen Jesus appears just in time, speaking the one word that exactly fits their need: PEACE. Their delight at seeing him is soon tempered with a spiritual maturity as he names their remarkable responsibility: Those you forgive *are* forgiven.

For Jesus to issue a mandate without giving his disciples all they need for the task would be out of character. So he provides the power that will make forgiveness possible: "Receive the Holy Spirit" (v. 22).

At the moment they felt his breath and knew his trust, their ministry and ours began. "What we *own*, we *owe*." The Spirit empowers us to offer peace where there is fear, acceptance where there is hate. Good ministry today reflects this commission of Jesus. We are faithful to it each time we respond with the gift of the Holy Spirit we have received.

Invitation to Group Sharing

1. Is there a time I was locked in fear like the disciples? What brought me peace?

2. Did I ever sense I used the Holy Spirit's gift of peace to free another from isolation or fear?

3. Do our parish ministries address the needs of people who lack peace or forgiveness? How can we improve?

4. How can we reach out to call forth the gifts of newcomers?

Invitation to Act

Determine a specific action (individual or group) that flows from your sharing. This should be your primary consideration. When choosing an individual action, determine what you will do and share it with the group. When choosing a group action, determine who will take responsibility for different aspects of the action. The following are secondary suggestions:

1. Next Sunday offer someone at Mass a sincere greeting of peace.

2. Spend some time with a friend, relative, neighbour or colleague who lacks self-esteem or finds it hard to forgive himself or herself. Let your care free that person.

3. At your family meal prayer, add a word of thanks for all the times the members of your family forgave each other.

Invitation to Closing Prayer

Give thanks to God (aloud or silently) for insights gained, for desires awakened, for directions clarified, for the gift of one another's openness and sensitivity. Conclude with the following:

Leader: For the gift of peace, we say,

All: Thank you, Spirit of Peace!

Leader: For the power to forgive, we say,

All: Thank you, Spirit of Love!

Leader: For the ministry we share, we say,

All: Thank you, Spirit of Compassion! Amen

Solemnity of the Most Holy Trinity

Faith: We Live within Mystery

Invitation to Pray
Pause for a few moments of silence and enter more deeply into the presence of God.

> ***Song:*** "Holy God, We Praise Thy Name," C A Walworth

> ***Proclaim the gospel:*** John 3:16-18
> Believing in Jesus Brings Eternal Life

Take a few minutes to savour a word, a phrase, a question, or a feeling that rises up in you. Reflect on this quietly or share it aloud.

Invitation to Reflect
Many Christians can recite the first verse of today's gospel. In fact, it is quoted often as a central belief and appears in many highly visible places these days. Still, the notion of God loving—not condemning—our world is a mystery we can hardly fathom. Maybe that is because WE don't have the eyes and hearts for it, so we continue selecting facets of our culture and people that please us. Ours is a much more discriminate relationship to the world than God's *full* love for it.

Our creed names God as Trinity, a community of three persons who live in loving communion. It is a community where mutuality,giving/receiving, and equality are enjoyed with no limits on time. This notion is so far from our experience, we call it a mystery. *Our* loves, after all, struggle to be mutual; our relationships are seldom equal; and we never seem to have enough time.

Today we are reminded that God the Father who loves the world and all its peoples gave his *only* Son so that we could come to believe. And this belief leads to the God-life that knows no limits. Who would not want a life like that?

Like a good parent who offers options and prays a child will choose the good, our heavenly Father offers us eternal life through faith in Jesus. Eternal life can begin now. We have a lifetime to ponder the mystery.

Invitation to Group Sharing

1. Have I ever been amazed, even baffled, by the deep love someone has for me? How did I respond?

2. What are some choices I have made that led to a fuller life? What were the consequences when I refused?

3. Does our parish community worship and minister in a way that reflects *our* love for the world God so loves?

4. Are there persons or groups in our parish who have experienced more judgment than acceptance? Is there a way we can begin to let them know they are full and worthy members of the world God loves?

Invitation to Act

Determine a specific action (individual or group) that flows from your sharing. This should be your primary consideration. When choosing an individual action, determine what you will do and share it with the group. When choosing a group action, determine who will take responsibility for different aspects of the action. The following are secondary suggestions:

1. Tell someone you love how you feel about him or her. When someone tells you he or she loves you, be open to receive and believe the message.

2. In family, work, or parish settings, catch yourself when you start to talk in condemning or judging ways. Do not join in when others do, either.

3. Place an index card with the words of John 3:16 on the mirror in your bathroom. See what this reminder does.

4. If you know someone who is troubled or depressed, suggest they talk to a parish team member about how to obtain help and advice.

Invitation to Closing Prayer

Give thanks to God (aloud or silently) for insights gained, for desires awakened, for directions clarified, for the gift of one another's open-

ness and sensitivity. Conclude with the following:

All: Loving God and Father,
                 your loving care for our world
                 and all its peoples
                 is beyond our understanding.
                 Lead us to believe in it and share it
                 so we and others will have the eternal life you promise.

                 We pray in Jesus' name and through the power of the
                 Holy Spirit. Amen

THE MOST HOLY BODY AND BLOOD OF THE LORD (CORPUS CHRISTI)

Eucharist: Where the Life Is!

Invitation to Pray
Pause for a few moments of silence and enter more deeply into the presence of God.

> *Song:* "O Bread of Heaven," St Alphonsus Liguori, Tr. E Vaughan

> *Proclaim the gospel:* John 6:51-58
> Jesus' Life: Source of Our Life

Take a few minutes to savour a word, a phrase, a question, or a feeling that rises up in you. Reflect on this quietly or share it aloud.

Invitation to Reflect
At best the people of Jesus' day received many of his teachings with caution. But today's gospel passage ranks among the highest for a sceptical reception. Listeners knew they needed bread to live. But many felt the life they had then was enough, was all there was. After all, they were descendents of Abraham and Sarah. So being told they didn't yet have real life within them was more than a red flag. Being invited to partake in their teacher's own flesh and blood in order to have life that would not end must have sounded far-fetched and even cannibalistic to some.

Yet the marvel of this teaching is that Jesus' word is true. The teacher himself models, even becomes, the teaching: Life that does not end is availableand it is found in me. No other rabbi could offer such intimacy to a follower. No other gesture has ever made such an impact on the life of believers in such a way.

Faith in a teaching comes from trust in the reliability of the teacher. All Jesus' other ministries, especially healing and telling about the Kingdom, brought life. His touch had returned people to health and returned them to family. His word freed and forgave. And if sharing in his life meant having these forever, the listening crowd could take a leap of faith again, for in Jesus they found someone on whom they could stake their lives.

Perhaps our key to a deepening faith in the Eucharist is learning to discover the many faces of Jesus giving us life in our daily healings and living of his Word. Then we will more fully experience the eternal life the Eucharist offers. For it is the summit of what life in Jesus can mean.

Invitation to Group Sharing

1. Is there someone whose life I would want to share forever, if I could? How could I make sure his or her life continues on with me somehow, even after he or she dies?

2. What is most meaningful or challenging to me in this gospel? Why?

3. How does my participation in the Eucharist deepen my life in Jesus in union with other believers? How has my faith in it as source of life developed since my first Holy Communion?

4. What are some ways our parish's manner of celebrating Eucharist enhances our faith in Jesus? How are my life and our life together as a parish being transformed by our weekly celebration of the Eucharist? How has community liturgy nourished me and challenged me to share Jesus' life with others? What will I do to express my gratitude?

Invitation to Act

Determine a specific action (individual or group) that flows from your sharing. This should be your primary consideration. When choosing an individual action, determine what you will do and share it with the group. When choosing a group action, determine who will take responsibility for different aspects of the action. The following are secondary suggestions:

1. Reach out in an inviting way to someone who has been away from the Eucharist for some time. During the coming week look for opportunities to reach out to those around you. Share with them the "bread" of joy, of listening, of compassion.

2. Next week at Sunday Mass, pray the words of the song during Communion with real intention. Be nourished in faith.

3. Next week at Sunday Mass, pay real attention to the eucharistic prayer. Share your reflections with a family member or friend.

4. Share a meal with those with whom you live. Begin with a table blessing and share some of the good things that happened to you during the day. Include references to the example of Jesus' life and the many times he shared meals with others. Talk about the Eucharist in the context of meal, of community.

5. If you bring Communion to the sick or housebound, share with them your personal love of the Eucharist.

Invitation to Closing Prayer
Give thanks to God (aloud or silently) for insights gained, for desires awakened, for directions clarified, for the gift of one another's openness and sensitivity. Conclude with the following:

Gracious God and Father,
we thank you for the gift of Jesus' life in Word,
in sacrament, and in the witness of those who believe.
We ask you to help us, who share in his life,
to be life for our world that hungers for the nourishment he is.

We pray through Jesus and in the Holy Spirit.
Amen

THE ASCENSION OF THE LORD

Jesus Calls Us to Make Disciples

Invitation to Pray
Pause for a few moments of silence and enter more deeply into the presence of God.

      Song: "I will be with you," Gerald Markland

      Proclaim the gospel: Matthew 28:16-20
                                 Teach and Baptise All Peoples

Take a few minutes to savour a word, a phrase, a question, or a feeling that rises up in you. Reflect on this quietly or share it aloud.

Invitation to Reflect
I had one teacher at school who told me I was a leader. She even encouraged me to become involved in the student government. And even though I did so and lost the election, I somehow believed her. I began to think of myself as a leader and pursued more responsibility at home and school. To this day, I am grateful that she helped me see the potential I had.

The disciples of Jesus were no different. They probably felt as inadequate as I to become leaders. And even after they had traveled with the master, told people what he could do for them, and tried their hand at healing, they still expected Jesus to take the lead, give the sign, and cajole them into greater faithfulness to the plan.

We, today and in this place, can say we have been claimed for ministry as well. Though the fulfillment of God's reign is closer today than when those first disciples received their call, so much more Good News is needed in our time. We are up to the task because our credentials are the best. We, too, have met the risen Jesus and worship him. We have known his presence every step of the way. We can go in peace, to love and serve the Lord.

Invitation to Group Sharing
    1. Has anyone ever seen potential in me that I could not see? How did that person's belief in me affect my behaviour or choices?

    2. What difference has it made that I was baptised? How do I share

the Good News of Jesus with the unique gifts I have?

3. What evidence is there that our parish community has authentically witnessed the Good News of Jesus? Through feedback from newcomers? In the results of our ministries? In those initiated at Easter? What more can we do?

Invitation to Act

Determine a specific action (individual or group) that flows from your sharing. This should be your primary consideration. When choosing an individual action, determine what you will do and share it with the group. When choosing a group action, determine who will take responsibility for different aspects of the action. The following are secondary suggestions:

1. Write a note to members of your parish involved in the Rite of Christian Initiation of Adults (RCIA), the Rite of Christian Initiation of Children (RCIC), or baptism classes for parents of infants. Thank them for their ministry of evangelisation on behalf of your Church community. (Offer to become a sponsor or catechist if you can.)

2. Next week at Mass, say the Creed with great conviction. Pay attention to and reflect on the phrases, "his kingdom will have no end" and "We acknowledge one baptism."

3. Show your respect for other baptised Christians. Attend an ecumenical event or ask a few friends what their baptism means to them.

4. Find a memento or photograph of your own or your children's baptism. Retell the story of that day. Pray that you and those who witnessed to the faith expressed that day will continue to grow in faith.

Invitation to Closing Prayer

Give thanks to God (aloud or silently) for insights gained, for desires awakened, for directions clarified, for the gift of one another's openness and sensitivity. Conclude with the following:

Leader: Let us begin our closing prayer with the sign in which we were baptised. In the name of the Father and of the Son and of the Holy Spirit.

All: Amen

Leader: Loving Father,
            today we celebrate together
            as a people claimed and named for you.
            We renew our commitment to be and
            to bring your Good News to those we meet,
            live with, and serve.
            We trust in your abiding presence
            and thank you for your love.
            In Jesus' name we pray.

All: Amen

Season of the Year
(Ordinary Time)

SECOND SUNDAY IN ORDINARY TIME

The Lamb of God

Invitation to Pray
Pause for a few moments of silence and enter more deeply into the presence of God.

> *Song:* "Behold the Lamb," Martin Willett

> *Proclaim the gospel:* John 1:29-34
> John the Baptist's Testimony about Jesus

Take a few minutes to savour a word, a phrase, a question, or a feeling that rises up in you. Reflect on this quietly or share it aloud.

Invitation to Reflect
John proclaims, "Behold the Lamb of God, who takes away the sin of the world" (v. 29). These words have become enshrined in the eucharistic invitation to share in the Lord's body and blood. But what an odd image! A Lamb of God.

This image recalls the servant so prominent in the Book of Isaiah who is led to the slaughter like a lamb (53:7). And it links Jesus with the lambs ritually slaughtered in preparation for the Passover meal (Exodus 12:21-27). In the Book of Revelation much is made of the Lamb who was slain (5:6) but now sits in triumph on the throne (22:1).

The image of Jesus as the Lamb of God must have had a powerful impact on early Christianity. A weak and passive animal is made the image of God's victory over sin and death. This would have contrasted markedly with those who longed for a warrior/king. Imagine how they would think: they thought they needed a super hero; they got a Lamb.

So often this is how God operates. Love is vulnerable. It does not coerce. It is available and faithful. Perhaps to counter our desire for a quick and final fix, God sends a Lamb as a sign that love takes time to heal, to win over, to triumph. The paradox of a helpless Lamb who triumphs catches our attention and forces us to wonder about how God really functions on our behalf. Yet we must never forget that it is this Lamb who takes away the sin of the world.

This Lamb is truly unique. The weak and vulnerable one emerges as the one who triumphs in power and the sin of the world is taken away. Our hearts are elated when we hear the prophet cry, "Behold the Lamb of God" (v. 29). In that moment, the weakness and foolishness of God to take away our sin become stronger than our need to hang on to our sin. A triumphant Lamb is indeed odd and rare, but so precious when we finally allow the Lamb to heal us.

Invitation to Group Sharing

1. What do you imagine a sheep or a lamb to be like? What is appealing about them? What is not? How does understanding this have an impact on my faith?

2. How confident am I in the power of vulnerable love to triumph in the end? Share some examples of the power of vulnerability that you have experienced.

3. How does Jesus, the Lamb of God, take away the sin of the world? How can we be vulnerable and allow the vulnerable Lamb to heal us?

Invitation to Act

Determine a specific action (individual or group) that flows from your sharing. This should be your primary consideration. When choosing an individual action, determine what you will do and share it with the group. When choosing a group action, determine who will take responsibility for different aspects of the action. The following are secondary suggestions:

1. Admit to yourself how scary it is to be vulnerable, to be like a lamb. Keep a note of your thoughts.

2. If possible, meet a need using less than your best talent. If you are in administration, sweep the floor. If you sweep the floor, volunteer to be on a committee doing some planning or decision making. Step outside your comfort zone and experience real vulnerability.

3. Find other images in Scripture and see how they can be used to help yourself and others discover how God works with us and for us.

4. Take some time this week to share your love with someone in a concrete way.

Invitation to Closing Prayer
Give thanks to God (aloud or silently) for insights gained, for desires awakened, for directions clarified, for the gift of one another's openness and sensitivity. Conclude with the following:

All recite together:

> Lamb of God, you take away the sins of the world:
>   have mercy on us.
>
> Lamb of God, you take away the sins of the world:
>   have mercy on us.
>
> Lamb of God, you take away the sins of the world:
>   grant us peace.
>
> Amen

THIRD SUNDAY IN ORDINARY TIME

Disciples

Invitation to Pray
Pause for a few moments of silence and enter more deeply into the presence of God.

> *Song:* "I Heard the Voice of Jesus Say," Horatius Bonar

> *Proclaim the gospel:* Matthew 4:12-23
> The Call of the First Disciples

Take a few minutes to savour a word, a phrase, a question, or a feeling that rises up in you. Reflect on this quietly or share it aloud.

Invitation to Reflect
Because the kingdom of heaven has come near, Jesus invites some fishermen to follow him. They immediately leave behind nets, boat and father, and follow Jesus. Just like that. Jesus has four companions with whom to share his ministry.

Despite his manifest power and his skill in speaking, Jesus is never a one-man show. The first executive decision he makes after his baptism and testing is to call a community into existence around the Word of God that he preaches.

This is in the best tradition of how God relates to us. God always calls a people. God enters into a covenant with 'us.' So around Jesus 'we' are formed.

We have to change to become part of this new people. We have to leave some things behind in order to embrace our new identity and purpose. Collectively these four leave nets, boat and father.

There is perhaps something symbolic about what the four left. Nets suggest that which we control. Nets capture and contain and limit. We may find our nets comforting since they give us an edge over what we can manipulate.

The boat represents our ability to come and go as we please. Boats allow us to be independent, unattached, floating, free and flexible. A boat can take us anywhere on the water.

One's father may be the stories and traditions we carry with us. We come from somewhere and from some people. These give us our identities and sense of who we are.

There's nothing wrong with nets and boats and fathers. They are essential to meet our needs for control and opportunity and roots. However when Jesus shows up with his announcement of God's transforming kingdom, we will have to give up some control, some opportunities, and some rooted-ness in order to be grasped by a reality not of our own making. Perhaps we leave nets and boats and fathers to have them given back to us again. We will still be in the family fishing business. Only what we fish for will change.

Invitation to Group Sharing

1. What are my nets? What gives me a sense of limit and control? What are some good things about nets? What are some problems with nets?

2. What is my boat? What gives me a sense of mobility, freedom, and options? What are some good things about boats? What are some problems with boats?

3. What or who are my 'fathers'? What or who tells my story and gives me identity? What are some good things about 'fathers'? What are some problems with 'fathers'?

4. What things do we have to give up and walk away from in order to approach and possess them anew? What will I do?

Invitation to Act

Determine a specific action (individual or group) that flows from your sharing. This should be your primary consideration. When choosing an individual action, determine what you will do and share it with the group. When choosing a group action, determine who will take responsibility for different aspects of the action. The following are secondary suggestions:

1. Imagine how it would feel to go fishing, catch a fish and let it go. Share how it might feel to pursue, capture and release another creature.

2. Reflect on and share about what it is about our faith that would act as 'bait' to attract those who are searching and questioning. Share your reflections with someone who is searching.

3. Participate in some evangelisation or catechetical ministry of your parish. Be part of an outreach that contacts and supports the spiritual search of others.

4. Listen to the stories of candidates and catechumens in the Rite of Christian Initiation process and discover how they see God active in their faith journey.

5. Become involved in an outreach to help victims of violence or natural disasters.

Invitation to Closing Prayer

Give thanks to God (aloud or silently) for insights gained, for desires awakened, for directions clarified, for the gift of one another's openness and sensitivity. Conclude with the following:

Father,
you come to us in our ordinary moments
to awaken us and call us toward a new reality
not of our own making.
Help us to be willing to let go of what we seem to control
in order to be claimed as disciples of your Son.
Let us have a share in your liberating and transforming ministry
through the power of the Holy Spirit. Amen

FOURTH SUNDAY IN ORDINARY TIME

How to Live

Invitation to Pray
Pause for a few moments of silence and enter more deeply into the presence of God.

> *Song:* "Blest Are The Pure of Heart," John Keble & W J Hall

> *Proclaim the gospel:* Matthew 5:1-12a
> The Beatitudes

Take a few minutes to savour a word, a phrase, a question, or a feeling that rises up in you. Reflect on this quietly or share it aloud.

Invitation to Reflect
Of all the teachings of Jesus, the beatitudes are among the most inspiring and the most challenging. Addressed to both the crowds and the disciples, this list represents the essence of how one lives out the covenant with God and others. This is where Torah (Law) and gospel meet to express a simple covenantal way of life that is still prophetically ahead of God's people calling us to respond in maturity, wholeness, and simple trust.

The beatitudes are about life and about how to live. All who can live them are called "blessed." Some translations have "happy." Commentators have remarked that the meaning is close to "congratulations," as if in living the beatitudes, one has come upon the deep secrets of how to live a human life. Perhaps we might even begin each beatitude with the phrase, "The most fully alive are" the poor in spirit, those who mourn, etc. The beatitudes are about life and about how to live it.

The Sermon on the Mount is always proclaimed as the gospel at Mass on the Feast of All Saints. The job description of a saint is not laid out in specifically religious or devotional or pietistic terms. Rather, a saint is one who willingly participates in poverty, mourning, and meekness, who hungers for justice, mercy and peace, who seeks integrity while enduring persecution for the sake of promoting the "uprightness" that Torah and Gospel describe.

This is a broad understanding of holiness and it says nothing about one's culture, race, gender, or age.

Participation in the reign of God is about the process of being transformed into the fullness of what it means to be a human person. The beatitudes describe what a fully mature human being looks like.

When we speak of human advancement we usually think in terms of intelligence or wealth or technology. God has a different definition of what an 'advanced' person would be like. We are not there yet. We still have work to do.

Invitation to Group Sharing

1. How do I understand my own advancement, my own transformation, in light of the gospel?

2. In what ways do the beatitudes call me to think in terms of gospel paradoxes strength in weakness, wisdom in foolishness, victory in failure, life in death? When have I seen these paradoxes in my life?

3. When have I felt that I was truly alive? Share an experience of such a time.

4. How can the beatitudes impact on my life to help me think of my Christian vocation as related to the needs of others and not just a matter of personal salvation?

Invitation to Act

Determine a specific action (individual or group) that flows from your sharing. This should be your primary consideration. When choosing an individual action, determine what you will do and share it with the group. When choosing a group action, determine who will take responsibility for different aspects of the action. The following are secondary suggestions:

1. Consider the future of humanity in terms of advancement in holiness and not just advancement in technology. What would it take for that to happen? Share one concrete action to help that advancement in holiness.

2. Try to participate in some bereavement ministry. Sit with and listen to those who mourn. Share their pain and come to befriend

your own.

3. If time permits, become involved in the work of some agency which works to make "upright" what has fallen and has been crushed.

4. The beatitudes represent a lifetime process of transformation. Pray for the grace to be so transformed.

Invitation to Closing Prayer
Give thanks to God (aloud or silently) for insights gained, for desires awakened, for directions clarified, for the gift of one another's openness and sensitivity. Conclude with the following:

Lord, help us not to fear
> poverty
> sorrow
> weakness
> hunger
> thirst

We find you in our emptiness.

Lord, help us to seek
> mercy
> courage
> peace
> uprightness

We serve you in our risk taking.

Lord, help us to endure
> persecution
> lies
> evil

We witness you in our struggle
and through it all we are blessed
as we are becoming more like you. Amen

Fifth Sunday in Ordinary Time

Witnesses to All the World

Invitation to Pray
Pause for a few moments of silence and enter more deeply into the presence of God.

> *Song:* "Gather Us In," Marty Haugen

> *Proclaim the gospel:* Matthew 5:13-16
> The Salt and the Light

Take a few minutes to savour a word, a phrase, a question, or a feeling that rises up in you. Reflect on this quietly or share it aloud.

Invitation to Reflect
Certainly, the beatitudes were startling to Jesus' audience. However, the words following the beatitudes are a more earthy and more easily understood challenge, offering guidance to his followers. Surely, they knew what being "the salt of the earth" (v. 13) was all about. Can you picture Jesus' followers, the next time they were using salt, remembering what he had said? Perhaps they once again reflected upon how they could add real flavour to their own lives and the lives of others—just as Jesus did.

The image of being "the light of the world" (v. 14) cannot be missed. We all know people who have truly been lights in our lives. We have thanked and praised God for bringing such people to us, especially in times of need, but have we truly expressed our gratitude to them?

Many think of religion as a totally personal, private endeavour. Although they might quietly do charity, being a witness to God's love, putting their light on a lamp stand where it gives light for all to see, is simply not part of their lifestyle. There is fear of sounding over-zealous or even fanatical. Yet the gospel is clear. Jesus is challenging his disciples to be witnesses to our heavenly Father.

We must consider how we can strive to keep our salty selves from going flat and to keep our lights shining on a hilltop. This requires that we become voices for love, mercy, and justice. We are called upon to be people of God's Kingdom, witnessing to our Lord in our families, in our neighbourhoods, and in our work environments.

106

Invitation to Group Sharing

1. In what ways do I consider the needs of all God's people in the decisions I make concerning my own and my family's lifestyle?

2. How have I experienced Jesus' challenge to let my light shine so that the goodness of my acts is recognised and the praise is given to God?

3. When we reflect upon the many blessings of our families and communities, how do we respond to God?

4. Would the people who know us think of us as salt or light? How can we provide flavour and light to others?

Invitation to Act

Determine a specific action (individual or group) that flows from your sharing. This should be your primary consideration. When choosing an individual action, determine what you will do and share it with the group. When choosing a group action, determine who will take responsibility for different aspects of the action. The following are secondary suggestions:

1. Reflect with your group on how different parts of your lives need salt and light. Be specific about changes, small and large, that could really be made.

2. Decide how you can be a witness to the Lord in your family, your circle of friends, your work environment, or your neighbourhood. Let your light shine.

3. Let someone who has been a light in your life know how much his or her light, his or her gifts have meant to you.

Invitation to Closing Prayer

Give thanks to God (aloud or silently) for insights gained, for desires awakened, for directions clarified, for the gift of one another's openness and sensitivity. Conclude with the following:

Dear Lord, open our hearts to the needs of your world.
Give us the courage to reach out beyond our comfortable lives
and to look into the suffering faces of your people.

We are grateful for the abundance of blessings you have given us.
We thank you for your continued love and mercy.
Strengthen us to act as your instruments of caring
in a world where injustice and a disregard
for the sacred human dignity of every person is often the rule.
Help us to truly be the "salt of the earth" (v. 13)
and "the light of the world" (v. 14) reaching out in the name of
Jesus our Lord. Amen

SIXTH SUNDAY IN ORDINARY TIME

Christian Morality

Invitation to Pray
Pause for a few moments of silence and enter more deeply into the presence of God.

> *Song:* "My God, Accept My Heart This Day," Matthew Bridges

> *Proclaim the gospel:* Matthew: 5:17-37
> Teaching about the Law

Take a few minutes to savour a word, a phrase, a question, or a feeling that rises up in you. Reflect on this quietly or share it aloud.

Invitation to Reflect
For centuries, the faithful Jewish nation followed the ancient Law of God's covenant proclaimed in the Old Testament. Jesus' teaching does not disregard the Law, but looks deeply into the fullness of its meaning. Jesus is very clear concerning the real justice of the law and the false justice and lack of inner holiness of certain scribes and Pharisees. Jesus' challenge to his listeners remains a challenge today. "…unless your righteousness surpasses that of the scribes and Pharisees, you will not enter the kingdom of heaven" (v. 20).

Like other Jewish teachers Jesus put a "hedge" or fence around each commandment so that people would not transgress. Jesus certainly was not minimising the horror of murder, but his exploration of the old Law surely strikes a far deeper note in the hearts of his listeners, and us. Anger, abusive, denigrating language, and contempt are most prevalent in modern life. Developing self-image in our children has become a major task for parents and teachers alike. Although Jesus doesn't use our modern terms, his interpretation of the Law certainly gets to the very heart of self-image and human relationships. We are advised not to approach the altar to offer our gifts if we are not in loving harmonious relationships with our brothers and sisters. Jesus condemns all those words and practices that do not uphold human dignity. Surely, good self-image for children or adults is impossible for those whose human dignity is crushed. What a startling challenge Jesus offers.

Jesus' teachings concerning adultery (including unfaithfulness in one's mind and heart) and divorce surely shocked any listeners who believed the letter of the law was what was necessary. Again Jesus is upholding the Law and human dignity. Jesus' language is terribly strong. Maim your body rather than be sinful in your heart. Quite clearly, Jesus is reminding us that sin may also be in one's attitude, one's motivation, not only in outward actions that may hide the evil in one's heart.

The final section of our gospel reading deals with the making of oaths. Certainly in our court system, we make oaths concerning the truthfulness of our statements. Sometimes a Bible is used; the words "so help me, God" are standard form. But again, Jesus looks for simplicity and clarity concerning our swearing of oaths. Just say the truth, speak without mental reservations or legal twists. Be trustworthy; speak from your heart. Say "yes" when you mean "yes" and "no" when you mean "no." Imagine how refreshing that would be in our everyday dealings with people.

Invitation to Group Sharing

1. When was I the victim of someone's anger, contempt, or abusive language. How did I feel? How did I handle the situation?

2. Sometimes we do not see how others are affected by our decisions. How would our lives and relationships change if we were more conscious of the God-given human dignity (self-image) of all the people we relate to every day?

3. How can we, as the people of God, promote attitudes within others and ourselves that truly promote the holiness Jesus requires of us all?

Invitation to Act

Determine a specific action (individual or group) that flows from your sharing. This should be your primary consideration. When choosing an individual action, determine what you will do and share it with the group. When choosing a group action, determine who will take responsibility for different aspects of the action. The following are secondary suggestions:

1. Make a positive effort to treat another with human dignity, especially someone to whom you may have been unkind. Decide how and when you will show respect to another person this week, for example, listen attentively when someone speaks, express appreciation, drive your car with regard for those around you.

2. Pray daily for God's grace to correct or strengthen your inner attitudes concerning one particular person.

3. Ask people you know how they would define Christian morality. Share your beliefs and learning with them.

Invitation to Closing Prayer
Give thanks to God (aloud or silently) for insights gained, for desires awakened, for directions clarified, for the gift of one another's openness and sensitivity. Conclude with the following:

Jesus, our Lord and Saviour,
you have given us yourself in Eucharist.
You are with us to strengthen us in our love for one another.
Help us acknowledge our need for change.

Your Gospel is our New Law, our New Covenant.
We need your help to change our lives
to be gospel people who truly live in love and holiness.
It is through your love that we can become who we are called to be.

We make our prayer united with you, the Spirit, and the Father.
Amen

SEVENTH SUNDAY IN ORDINARY TIME

Love Your Enemies

Invitation to Pray
Pause for a few moments of silence and enter more deeply into the presence of God.

> *Song:* "Bless the Lord, my soul," Taizé

> *Proclaim the gospel:* Matthew 5:38-48
> Teaching about Retaliation

Take a few minutes to savour a word, a phrase, a question, or a feeling that rises up in you. Reflect on this quietly or share it aloud.

Invitation to Reflect
G. K. Chesterton, the famous author and convert said, "It is not that Christianity has failed, it is that it has never been tried." When we hear the well-known command, "Love your enemies and pray for those who perse-cute you" (v. 44), we must admit that Chesterton is at least partially right. Religious wars, ethnic cleansing, and racial prejudice include Christians all over the world. Although for years Catholics prayed for the conversion of Russia, very little praying for the persecutors of the modern world is includ-ed in our liturgical or private prayer. Yet " …he makes his sun rise on the bad and the good and causes rain to fall on the just and the unjust" (v. 45). Jesus' words are incredibly focused. Loving our enemies and praying for those who oppress us provide the real proof that we are God's people. Imagine the reaction of Jesus' listeners when our Lord told the crowds that those who are his followers must turn the other cheek (v. 39), go the extra mile (v. 41), and answer the call of the beggar (v. 42).

These few lines are probably among the most challenging in the gospel. We, as a Church, have not always been the best models for non-resistance and real love of our enemies. Yet, the many examples of Catholic charities toward the needy of our world certainly point to a real awareness of Jesus' command. We, as a Church, as God's people, do reach out to the poor of the world. Catholics are among the world's most generous. Yet, have we really taken to heart Jesus' command to love with a love so strong that we are willing to actually love those who have hurt us? "Charity begins at home" is not part of the gospel. It is nowhere in the Bible. If this saying means that love is learned and first shared within our homes and families, it is surely commendable, but if it means to help only those who are your own, then it seems to contradict Jesus' words in the gospel. "If you love those who love you, what recompense will you have?" (v. 46).

It is relatively easy to be good to those who love you. And it is rather difficult to be good to those who do not love you, maybe even hate you. But Jesus was quite specific. His commandment demands we love far beyond our own families and friends. It is truly how we love God. If we are all made in the image and likeness of God, we simply cannot hate, denigrate, or oppress anyone.

Many people from the East bow when they greet someone. The bow, which looks like a gesture of respect or subservience, is acknowledging the Divine in every person. The bow speaks an awareness that God dwells in every one. It is an eastern genuflection, a good reminder of God's presence and an invitation to treat others as God's family.

Invitation to Group Sharing

1. How specifically do I respond to Jesus' command, "So be perfect, just as your heavenly Father is perfect" (v. 48)? Keep in mind that God's perfection means being complete through love.

2. Without indicating names, share about a time when you changed your attitude toward someone you considered unlovable by trying to love him or her.

3. In our modern world how do I understand "turn the other cheek"? (see v. 39). Have I ever experienced someone turning the other cheek and offering no resistance to injuries or unkindness that I may have caused? Explain.

Invitation to Act

Determine a specific action (individual or group) that flows from your sharing. This should be your primary consideration. When choosing an individual action, determine what you will do and share it with the group. When choosing a group action, determine who will take responsibility for different aspects of the action. The following are secondary suggestions:

1. After prayer and reflection, be especially loving toward someone or a group of people to whom you have been unloving.

2. As a group, research the history of a modern religious war, ethnic cleansing, or racial prejudice. Determine how love and/or non-resistance could change the situation. What will we do? Share your reflections next week.

3. Make a specific commitment to acknowledge the image of God in all the people in your world.

4. Be truly present to a family member, a colleague, or a neighbour this week. Listen with your heart to the needs of this person.

Invitation to Closing Prayer

Give thanks to God (aloud or silently) for insights gained, for desires awakened, for directions clarified, for the gift of one another's openness and sensitivity. Conclude with the following:

God our Father,
we give you thanks that we are made in your image and likeness.
Help us be very aware of your presence in all your people.
Give us the courage to treat all as we would treat Jesus.

We ask that your Holy Spirit open our hearts
and teach us about your love and our need to love others.
We truly desire to live Jesus' commands,
but are painfully aware that we cannot do it
without the help of your Spirit.
We ask this through our Lord and Saviour, Jesus Christ.
Amen

Eighth Sunday in Ordinary Time

Trust/Christian Stewardship

Invitation to Pray
Pause for a few moments of silence and enter more deeply into the presence of God.

> *Song:* "O God, You Search Me," Bernadette Farrell

> *Proclaim the gospel:* Matthew 6:24-34
> Trust in Divine Providence

Take a few minutes to savour a word, a phrase, a question, or a feeling that rises up in you. Reflect on this quietly or share it aloud.

Invitation to Reflect
For most of us, tension and anxiety can be great. All our technology and the conveniences of modern life have not made our daily lives easy. Worries and fears cause emotional and physical health problems that sap our lives of joy and peace. How many people do we know who are truly content, satisfied with their lives? Sadly, the numbers are small, while the numbers of those suffering depression are rising. Statistics of suicide, even teenage suicide, are a frightening commentary on today's society.

Jesus has a message for all of us who are consumed by our fears and anxieties. "Do not worry about your life" (v. 25) and even harder to hear, "You cannot be the slave of both God and of money" (v. 24). How are we to respond to these words? Surely, Jesus knows we must support our families and have money to pay our bills. But are we giving ourselves to the *pursuit* of money? Are we satisfied or are we forever accumulating more possessions, greater luxuries? Do we judge others by their possessions? Do we feel powerful because we have money?

This gospel asks for the deep trust of people of faith who truly believe that God's love and care provide for all our needs. One of the keys to this gospel passage may be Jesus' advice. "Seek first the kingdom of God and his righteousness, and all these things will be given you besides" (v. 33). Perhaps if we were seeking only God's way, "...your kingdom come, your will be done" (Matthew 6:10), we would be able to find real joy and contentment in our lives, and understand clearly God's call to us to share our

115

abundance with those in need.

We do know that God does not want the human family to suffer hunger. Toward the end of Matthew's Gospel, Jesus clearly tells us that those who have fed, clothed, and comforted the needy will receive God's blessing and inherit the kingdom, and those who have not cared for others will not be with God (Matthew 25:31-46).

In our modern world, our faith should enable us to trust in God's care and to become instruments of God's care for others. God will use us in helping others to know is love and care. We, God's Church, are called beyond self-concern, to be the hands and heart of God in his world.

Invitation to Group Sharing

1. Through any given day, what are my greatest worries? How does my trust in God affect these anxieties?

2. How do I understand the care of our heavenly Father? Have I experienced God's care?

3. What can we do to reduce the anxieties of the people we are with everyday? Does our faith and trust in God provide a light of strength for others?

4. What is the role of our Christian community and our parish concerning the lessons of this gospel? What are the central concerns of our small Christian community/parish? Do we need to get our priorities straight, especially in my personal life?

Invitation to Act

Determine a specific action (individual or group) that flows from your sharing. This should be your primary consideration. When choosing an individual action, determine what you will do and share it with the group. When choosing a group action, determine who will take responsibility for different aspects of the action. The following are secondary suggestions:

1. Spend five to ten minutes each day asking God to take away your fears and anxieties and help you live in his peace.

2. Make a concrete attempt to simplify your life, your concerns about money, accumulations of possessions, food, and clothing.

Buy less, give away more.

3. Organise a food and/or clothing drive, and as a group, bring these items to those in need. Find joy in sharing yourself and your possessions.

Invitation to Closing Prayer

Give thanks to God (aloud or silently) for insights gained, for desires awakened, for directions clarified, for the gift of one another's openness and sensitivity. Conclude with the following:

Leader: For all the times, Lord, when we have put our desire for money and possessions above our relationship with you, we pray,

All: Lord, have mercy.

Leader: For all the times we have considered ourselves better than others because of our wealth or education, we pray,

All: Lord, have mercy.

Leader: For all the times we have been selfish and turned away from the needs of others, we pray,

All: Lord, have mercy.

Leader: For all the times we have worried over what we would eat, drink, or wear, we pray,

All: Lord, have mercy.

Pray the Lord's Prayer together listening deeply to the words Jesus taught us.

NINTH SUNDAY IN ORDINARY TIME

Practicing Like a Wise Person

Invitation to Pray
Pause for a few moments of silence and enter more deeply into the presence of God.

> *Song:* "The Church's One Foundation," S J Stone

> *Proclaim the gospel:* Matthew 7:21-27
> The True Disciple

Take a few minutes to savour a word, a phrase, a question, or a feeling that rises up in you. Reflect on this quietly or share it aloud.

Invitation to Reflect
So much has been written on doing God's will. Often we Catholics have assured ourselves that 'church on Sunday' and 'getting one's sacraments' are the essence of doing God's will. Without doubt our liturgy and our sacraments are great gifts to us. Celebrating with the Christian community is certainly a major means of strength. Our participation in liturgy and sacraments is the foundation of our lives, the bedrock that makes it possible for us to do God's will. However, Jesus is clearly telling us that simply crying out, "Lord, Lord" (v. 21), is not the heart of his message. The word of the gospel is far deeper than religious worship. Jesus does not seem to be impressed with the prophecy in his name, or exorcising devils, or even performing miracles. Yet, we still desire signs and wonders and we flock to sightings of what some have deemed miraculous.

The key to this challenging passage is hearing the words of the Lord and putting them into practice. If we only hear the words and do not live them, we are the foolish who build on sand. At Mass, before the gospel is read, we pray as we cross ourselves three times, that the Word of God be in our minds, on our lips, and in our hearts. This prayer, often done without much real thought, is truly asking the help of God's Spirit to live the Word of God, to put it into practice every day of our lives. This is doing God's will.

Not one of us wants to have the winds and rain destroy our houses, yet the torrents of life sometimes blow the words of our Lord from our hearts and minds. Jesus tells us to put his words into practice, and to make the 'Sunday experience' the rock foundation of our lives.

118

Invitation to Group Sharing

1. I am told to build wisely on a rock foundation. What is the rock foundation of my life?

2. What do I think of when I reflect on Jesus' message in this reading? What words do I find difficult to live by? Be specific.

3. What could we do to strengthen our total commitment to the words of Jesus?

4. How can we help others live the gospel and know the security of a rock foundation?

Invitation to Act

Determine a specific action (individual or group) that flows from your sharing. This should be your primary consideration. When choosing an individual action, determine what you will do and share it with the group. When choosing a group action, determine who will take responsibility for different aspects of the action. The following are secondary suggestions:

1. Read from one of the gospels each day and try to put the message into your life.

2. List for yourself the words of Jesus that offer the most challenge to you. Pray for the strength to make them part of your life and work to put them into practice.

3. Consider being a reader at Mass to proclaim the Word of God to others.

4. Support those who build affordable housing for all in need.

Invitation to Closing Prayer
Give thanks to God (aloud or silently) for insights gained, for desires awakened, for directions clarified, for the gift of one another's openness and sensitivity. Conclude with the following:

Lord Jesus, you speak to our hearts in the gospel message. Please strengthen our wills to put your message into practice.

Leader:	"As I have loved you, so you also should love one another" (John 13:34).
All:	Help us, Lord, to live your words.
Leader	"Forgive us our debts, as we forgive our debtors" (Matthew 6:12).
All:	Help us, Lord, to live your words.
Leader:	"For I was hungry and you gave me food...ill and you cared for me" (Matthew 25:35, 36).
All:	Help us, Lord, to live your words.
Leader:	"Stop judging" (Matthew 7:1).
All:	Help us, Lord, to live your words.
Leader:	"You cannot serve God and mammon" (Matthew 6:24).
All:	Help us, Lord, to live your words.
Leader:	"You are the light of the world" (Matthew 5:14).
All:	Help us, Lord, to live your words.

TENTH SUNDAY IN ORDINARY TIME

Concern for the Neglected

Invitation to Pray
Pause for a few moments of silence and enter more deeply into the presence of God.

> *Song:* "Lay Your Hands," Carey Landry

> *Proclaim the gospel:* Matthew 9:9-13
> "Follow Me."

Take a few minutes to savour a word, a phrase, a question, or a feeling that rises up in you. Reflect on this quietly or share it aloud.

Invitation to Reflect
We are usually taken aback when we reflect upon the situations in this part of Matthew's Gospel. Of all the people around him, why did Jesus choose Matthew, a tax collector? To this day, we are not very fond of tax collectors. We are happy to connect and even identify tax collectors with sinners. Yet, when Jesus has dinner at Matthew's home, many such sinners join him. Jesus welcomes these people, stopping the nasty criticism of the Pharisees by explaining that "those who are well do not need a physician, but the sick do" (v. 12). Although we may feel superior at times to public criminals, drug dealers, and murderers, there are few among us who would claim we are not sinners.

The end of the gospel passage reiterates a common scriptural theme. Jesus is quoting the prophet Hosea when he tells the Pharisees that they must learn the meaning of the words, "I desire mercy, not sacrifice" (v. 13 quoting Hosea 6:6). Jesus' challenge must have startled his listeners who were most conscious of performing the proper ritual sacrifices. His words challenge us yet today. We have separated ourselves from many of God's people through snobbery and racism. The Church sometimes has sinned by treating people of means and power with more respect than the oppressed and downtrodden. The Church at times has sinned by treating people of different racial backgrounds with inequality. *We* are the Church!

Mercy is what Jesus desired, and mercy is what Jesus gave to all when he walked upon the earth. We, the Church, are called to act as Christ, and be merciful people. Shakespeare, in his play *The Merchant of Venice,* speaks of mercy, saying:

> "The quality of mercy is not strained. It droppeth as the gentle rain from heaven upon the place beneath. It is twice blest: It blesseth him that gives and him that takes."

Shakespeare understood that mercy is love flowing from one person to another, enriching both the giver and the receiver. Mercy is what we count on in our relationship with God. We know clearly that we will depend on God's loving mercy when we receive divine judgment.

Invitation to Group Sharing

1. Am I aware of times I have judged others by their class or race, religion or intelligence? Share your experience.

2. When have I experienced the outpouring of God's loving mercy in my life?

3. How can I become a more merciful, less judgmental person? Who can help me with this?

4. How can we work toward the elimination of snobbery, racism, and sexism in our lives?

Invitation to Act

Determine a specific action (individual or group) that flows from your sharing. This should be your primary consideration. When choosing an individual action, determine what you will do and share it with the group. When choosing a group action, determine who will take responsibility for different aspects of the action. The following are secondary suggestions:

1. Each day this week, resolve to ask God's mercy upon your sinfulness and God's help in offering mercy to others.

2. Make a concerted effort each day this week to act with mercy toward someone.

3. As a group, investigate incidents of racism or snobbery that still exist in schools, neighbourhoods, workplaces, or even parishes. What action can we take to address and alleviate the racism or snobbery?

4.   Thank God for the people in your life who have shown mercy or compassion to you.

Invitation to Closing Prayer

Give thanks to God (aloud or silently) for insights gained, for desires awakened, for directions clarified, for the gift of one another's openness and sensitivity. Conclude with the following:

Leader: For all the times we have been self-righteous,

All: Lord, have mercy upon us.

Leader: For all the times we have judged others according to outward appearances,

All: Lord, have mercy upon us.

Leader: For all the times we have treated people without mercy and justice because of their sex, race, or class,

All: Lord, have mercy upon us.

All: Lord, help us to understand your responses to the self-righteous and learn the meaning of the words, "I desire mercy, not sacrifice" (v. 13).

ELEVENTH SUNDAY IN ORDINARY TIME

Christian Vocation

Invitation to Pray
Pause for a few moments of silence and enter more deeply into the presence of God.

> *Song:* "Here I Am, Lord," Daniel L. Schutte, SJ

> *Proclaim the gospel*: Matthew 9:36—10:8
> Mission of the Twelve

Take a few minutes to savour a word, a phrase, a question, or a feeling that rises up in you. Reflect on this quietly or share it aloud.

Invitation to Reflect
Almost daily on our television news we see suffering crowds of people. They are the victims of war, ethnic cleansing, floods, or famine. Millions of God's people are refugees without decent human housing and food. Among these crowds are millions of children, child labourers, child prostitutes, the restavecs of Haiti (children of the desperate poor sold to rich families as servants), and the abandoned baby girls of China. The gospel tell us that when he sees the crowds Jesus' heart is moved with compassion. (v. 36). Just as he called his apostles, Jesus is calling us to be labourers for the harvest, to have compassion on the world's suffering people.

Our Church has a long history of missionary work. Members of religious orders and lay women and men have given their lives to witness to Christ's message. And in this missionary endeavour, believers have worked for human dignity, against indecent housing, poor sanitation, and disease (the lepers and demons of our day). We think of the contemporary Christian martyrs of southern Sudan and India; the Jesuit fathers, the sisters, and Christian people of Central America who are modern-day martyrs. All of these people were moved by the same faith and compassion that touched the heart of our Lord.

Certainly, not all compassionate believers are able to become missionaries in other lands. However, our prayers, understanding, compassion, and financial support can be with them; but labourers are also needed at home. All baptised Christians have a vocation to be other Christs in the world, to be apostles. While the apostles had a special role in the early Church, we know that all Christians, men and women, through the centuries have witnessed to Christ's mission. They have laboured among the people of God as teachers, prophets, musicians, healers, preachers, and writers. They have also been ordinary people of faith whose very lives have announced that "the kingdom of heaven is at hand" (v. 7). Faith engenders faith. Jesus' words to his apostles and to us are very clear, "Without cost you have received; without cost you are to give" (v. 8).

Invitation to Group Sharing

1. Who are the people I encounter who are without material resources or without religious faith? How do I respond to them?

2. Where and how could I be a labourer for Christ's harvest?

3. What could we, as a group, specifically do about the needs of our world's suffering?

Invitation to Act

Determine a specific action (individual or group) that flows from your sharing. This should be your primary consideration. When choosing an individual action, determine what you will do and share it with the group. When choosing a group action, determine who will take responsibility for different aspects of the action. The following are secondary suggestions:

1. Read about a modern-day saint and/or apostle. Try to imitate the virtues of that person.

2. Talk to a person without religious faith. Simply tell him or her why you believe and how your faith impacts upon your lifestyle.

3. Research the needs of one group of the world's suffering, for example, refugees, prisoners, abused children, homeless people. Decide how you can be an instrument of healing.

4. Contact someone who has ministered to you in your need and thank him or her.

Invitation to Closing Prayer

Give thanks to God (aloud or silently) for insights gained, for desires awakened, for directions clarified, for the gift of one another's openness and sensitivity. Conclude with the following:

Lord, we know we are called to be apostles,
labourers for your harvest.
We have been blessed in so many ways,
and most importantly,
with the gift of faith.
Help us always to be aware
of all those who suffer daily,
especially those who are
without the loving support
of family and friends.
Strengthen us to be your compassionate
hands and heart,
unafraid to share our lives and our faith in you.
We ask this in your name.
Amen

TWELFTH SUNDAY IN ORDINARY TIME

Courage and Fortitude as Disciples

Invitation to Pray
Pause for a few moments of silence and enter more deeply into the presence of God.

> *Song:* "You Shall Cross the Barren Desert," Robert J. Dufford, SJ

> *Proclaim the gospel:* Matthew 10:26-33
> Courage in Difficulty

Take a few minutes to savour a word, a phrase, a question, or a feeling that rises up in you. Reflect on this quietly or share it aloud.

Invitation to Reflect
In this part of Matthew's Gospel, the author continues Jesus' instruction to the apostles he is sending out to spread the Good News. Although Jesus has told them they are being sent like "sheep in the midst of wolves" (Matthew 10:16), he implores them not to fear "those who kill the body but cannot kill the soul" (v. 28).

Throughout the history of our Church, faithful believers have followed Christ in their refusal to sacrifice the truth in order to protect their own lives. In the Middle Ages, St Joan of Arc was burned at the stake, a consequence of her unwavering faith and courage. St Thomas More was beheaded for his unbending loyalty to the Holy Father's judgment against King Henry VIII. In our own times, Archbishop Oscar Romero, the Voice of the Voiceless in San Salvador, was assassinated at Mass for his courage against an evil and unjust military government.

These martyrs truly lived this gospel. Their human fear of bodily harm did not govern their lives. Truth, justice, their personal integrity, and the care of their souls were their real priorities. Surely these martyrs and many, many others through the centuries acknowledged Christ, confident that Christ would acknowledge them before God.

Jesus assures his apostles that they truly have nothing to fear. He uses wonderful imagery to explain the intensity of God's love and care for each one of us. "Every hair on your head are counted" (v. 30). Our Creator's total and unending concern for all creation—"not [a single sparrow] falls to the ground without your Father's knowledge" (v. 29)—assures us of our place within the heart of God. The Lord's love for each one of us is greater, more intimate than even the love parents have for their children. In return for this incredible gift of loving care, we are simply asked to fear not, to trust, and to acknowledge before the world that our God is the God of love.

Invitation to Group Sharing

1. Do I truly believe that God knows me with the great intimacy of "counting every hair"? How do I respond?

2. Do I think of myself as a courageous disciple for Christ? Why or why not?

3. Since life is so precious to us, how can we "not be afraid of those who kill the body" (v. 28)?

4. Who are those who can destroy both body and soul? How can we prevent this destruction?

Invitation to Act

Determine a specific action (individual or group) that flows from your sharing. This should be your primary consideration. When choosing an individual action, determine what you will do and share it with the group. When choosing a group action, determine who will take responsibility for different aspects of the action. The following are secondary suggestions:

1. Research organisations in your area that work against the destruction of the body and soul (organisations that work for peace, pro-life organisations, prison ministries, and drug, alcohol, gambling abuse. Get involved in an organisation working to end these destructive forces.

2. Reflect prayerfully and make a list of all those people or situations in your life that can weaken your integrity. Determine an action you will take.

3. Decide on a positive action you will take to acknowledge Christ before others.

4. Take some time to look at the birds and reflect on how much

God cares for them. Speak in gratitude from your heart to God for his loving care for you.

Invitation to Closing Prayer

Give thanks to God (aloud or silently) for insights gained, for desires awakened, for directions clarified, for the gift of one another's openness and sensitivity. Conclude with the following:

Leader: Lord, your love for us is overwhelming. The very hairs on our head are counted, yet we ignore the needs of others.

All: Lord, give us the courage to speak and act in your name.

Leader: You have guided us toward goodness and life despite our unfaithfulness.

All: Lord, give us the courage to speak and act in your name.

Leader: The power of the world often is the voice to which we turn.

All: Lord, give us the courage to speak and act in your name.

Leader: We are a fearful people, often lacking in faith and trust in you.

All: Lord, give us the courage to speak and act in your name.

All: You are our loving Father. We rejoice in your compassionate concern for us. Help us to show compassion to the people in our world. With the help of your Holy Spirit, we will be your witnesses. We pray in Jesus' name.
Amen

THIRTEENTH SUNDAY IN ORDINARY TIME

Take up Your Cross

Invitation to Pray

Pause for a few moments of silence and enter more deeply into the presence of God.

> *Song:* "Servant Song," Rory Cooney
>
> *Proclaim the gospel:* Matthew 10:37-42
> Discipleship

Take a few minutes to savour a word, a phrase, a question, or a feeling that rises up in you. Reflect on this quietly or share it aloud.

Invitation to Reflect

The final words of Jesus' instructions to his disciples before they begin their mission express the very heart of the Christian message. Matthew's Gospel, written some years after the crucifixion, has Jesus speaking of the cross. "Whoever does not take up his cross and follow after me is not worthy of me" (v. 38). The crucifixion of Jesus became the central event for the people of Matthew's community. They came to understand that Jesus gave his life for them, for the truth, the integrity of God's message. Jesus accepted the cross with all its horror, rather than compromise his truth, his love for the Father and for them. The people of Matthew's community understood that Jesus was willing to sacrifice his life for others.

Our faith asks us to follow Jesus and to seek to do God's will. We are not to put our own desires first. To be worthy of the Lord requires selflessness, a death to self. And it is in this death that we will live, just as in Jesus' death he found new life. "Whoever finds his life will lose it, and whoever loses his life for my sake will find it" (v. 39).

The promises of our Lord challenge us, but also offer us great reward. So many times in the Scriptures Jesus does not glorify "religious leaders." The reward received by a prophet or holy person is not much compared to the promised reward of Jesus if only we give "a cup of cold water to one of these little ones" (v. 42). Once again, Matthew points out Jesus' concern for the lowly.

In the Old Testament, God is often described as a jealous God. This jealousy is a divine emotion that demands that love of God be the centre of our lives. We are reminded of this when we read that if we love mother, father, son, or daughter more than we love our Lord, we are not worthy of him. Certainly, Jesus is not against familial love, but he requires the love of the Lord to be primary.

Invitation to Group Sharing

1. The world tells me I should be concerned about myself, be number one. How do I reconcile this with the gospel injunction to lose my life for Jesus' sake? How do I follow Jesus' command to take up my cross?

2. Is it possible for us to put the love of our Lord before the love of our family? How do I love in the way Jesus demands? Share some examples.

3. As a community, when have we looked for the rewards given to prophets and holy ones, rather than serving the lowly in God's name? What will we do to serve in a more selfless way?

Invitation to Act

Determine a specific action (individual or group) that flows from your sharing. This should be your primary consideration. When choosing an individual action, determine what you will do and share it with the group. When choosing a group action, determine who will take responsibility for different aspects of the action. The following are secondary suggestions:

1. With God's grace, determine to take up a cross being presented to you.

2. Telephone, visit, or write to someone you know whose cross is particularly painful. As best you can, offer him or her words of encouragement.

3. As a group, interview members of your parish staff, asking them to describe how their discipleship/ministry has helped them become who they are.

4. Take time to write a description of yourself as a disciple of Jesus.

5. This week, speak with someone from whom you are estranged, go shopping for someone who is confined, or listen to someone whom you do not particularly like.

Invitation to Closing Prayer

Give thanks to God (aloud or silently) for insights gained, for desires awakened, for directions clarified, for the gift of one another's openness and sensitivity. Conclude with the following:

Left: We are loved by our God,
yet we often love poorly.
Show us the way, Lord.

Right: You have made us your sisters and brothers,
yet we often ignore the crosses of our sisters and brothers
in God's human family.
Show us the way, Lord.

Left: Although you accept us as we are,
we often do not accept others or ourselves.
Show us the way, Lord.

Right: You have showered upon us life's blessings,
yet we often refuse to help the needy.
Show us the way, Lord.

All: Dear God, give us a new perspective.
Help us look at the world
through the eyes of Jesus the Christ,
and be truly willing to take up our crosses and
follow him.
Amen

FOURTEENTH SUNDAY IN ORDINARY TIME

Take up the Yoke of Jesus

Invitation to Pray
Pause for a few moments of silence and enter more deeply into the presence of God.

> *Song:* "O Let All Who Thirst," John Foley, SJ

> *Proclaim the gospel:* Matthew 11:25-30
> Praise of the Father

Take a few minutes to savour a word, a phrase, a question, or a feeling that rises up in you. Reflect on this quietly or share it aloud.

Invitation to Reflect
Jesus himself is praising and thanking God for the revelation given to him. This revelation proclaims that "…although you have hidden these things from the wise and the learned you have revealed them to little ones" (v. 25). The "wise and the learned" among the Jews of Jesus' time were the Pharisees and the Sadducees, the religious leaders and scholars and interpreters of the Law.

Jesus was able to receive everything from the Father, for his heart and mind were totally open to the will of God. Jesus was without personal desires; he had no agenda of his own. Jesus was not interested in his own glory, but only that of God. His humility was complete. And humility is truth.

In our lives, we reveal ourselves to very few people. We reveal ourselves only to those who completely accept and love us. We hold back the deep, sacred truth in our lives from all those who could use that truth against us, or mock our self-revelation. When Jesus speaks of his relationship with the Father, we learn of a relationship of complete love and trust, a relationship of oneness. Although Jesus is part of the human race, he is God's own Son, for he desires only what God desires. His will is pure, and he is God with us (see Matthew 1:23). Through Jesus, we learn of God, for he has revealed God's truth and God's way to us, the merest of children. Our own desires and our own life agendas prevent us from knowing and accepting the fullness of divine truth.

Certainly all people have known the weariness and burdens of life. Jesus is inviting us to be one with him and to learn his gentleness and his heart's humility. Knowing what God wishes to reveal to our hearts would lighten our burdens and give rest to our souls. To find this rest, we must be willing to accept Jesus, who is eager not only to share our burdens, but also to bring us to the love of the Father.

Invitation to Group Sharing

1. What revelations of the gospel are the greatest challenges in my life? How do I respond?

2. What person in my life can I confide in easily? Who holds me in confidence? What are the qualities of those to whom I reveal myself?

3. How do I turn to Jesus when I am suffering the burdens and weariness of life? Share.

4. How can we, as individuals and as a group, spread the Good News that God has revealed to us?

Invitation to Act

Determine a specific action (individual or group) that flows from your sharing. This should be your primary consideration. When choosing an individual action, determine what you will do and share it with the group. When choosing a group action, determine who will take responsibility for different aspects of the action. The following are secondary suggestions:

1. Visit someone in the hospital or a nursing home who may be weary or heavily burdened.

2. Be one with Jesus by specifically lightening the burden of someone you know by offering help or support.

3. Read the gospel for this week slowly and reflectively. Reflect prayerfully about your own actual acceptance and living of gospel revelation.

4. Take some time this week to rest in the Lord.

Invitation to Closing Prayer

Give thanks to God (aloud or silently) for insights gained, for desires awakened, for directions clarified, for the gift of one another's openness and sensitivity. Conclude with the following:

Dear God, we praise and thank you
for Jesus who is your Word, your revelation.
Please help us to open our hearts,
our minds, and our lives
to your truth and your way.
Help us to accept our own burdens
and to be willing to work toward
easing the burdens of others.

We believe our lives will be easy
and our burdens light
if we are joined to your Son,
who is gentle and humble of heart.
Thank you for this great Incarnation of your love!

In Jesus' name we pray.
Amen

FIFTEENTH SUNDAY IN ORDINARY TIME

Parable of the Sower and the Seed

Invitation to Pray
Pause for a few moments of silence and enter more deeply into the presence of God.

> *Song:* "Unless a Grain of Wheat," Bernadette Farrell

> *Proclaim the gospel:* Matthew 13:1-23
> Planted and Rooted in God

Take a few minutes to savour a word, a phrase, a question, or a feeling that rises up in you. Reflect on this quietly or share it aloud.

Invitation to Reflect
A biblical scholar, C. H. Dodd, offers the classic definition of a parable:

> "At its simplest, the parable is a metaphor of common life,
> arresting the hearer by its vividness or strangeness, and leav-
> ing the mind in sufficient doubt about its precise application
> to tease it into active thought."

Jesus very often taught the crowds in parables. In this passage, he explains to his disciples why he chooses to teach in this way. He even quotes the prophet Isaiah, who was also troubled about the lack of in-depth understanding of the people to whom he prophesied. Parables offer deep truth in story form. They allow the hearers (readers) to judge for themselves where they fit in the story.

Jesus is the master teacher. His word is offered to us. Each person who has heard the word will receive it in his or her own way. Jesus, the sower, generously plants the seeds, but the rest is up to us. Only the words of our Lord that are accepted deep within us will have lasting effect. Any person who has worked in a garden to grow flowers or vegetables knows the peril of the seed that does not find itself in good, rich soil.

It is so easy to have good initial intentions to follow the Word of God, but the world is rarely a nurturing place. Trials and temptations confront us daily. Jesus is completely aware of the many pulls and distractions of our lives. He knows the presence and power of evil. He is so painfully aware that even his Good News depends on our acceptance. He sows the seed with love, knowing the greatness of his message. "But blessed are your eyes, because they see, and your ears, because they hear" (v. 16). As difficult as it may be to hold fast to the Word of God, those seeds that take root in our hearts, Jesus assures us, will bring blessings "a hundred or sixty or thirtyfold" (v. 23).

Invitation to Group Sharing

1. What seed of God's Word is firmly planted in my heart and significant in my daily life? What seed of God's Word needs greater nurturing in my life?

2. What or who are the rocky ground, thin soil, or thorns of my life?

3. How can we, as a community, truly hear the Lord's message in our lives and offer it to other people? What specific action will we take?

Invitation to Act

Determine a specific action (individual or group) that flows from your sharing. This should be your primary consideration. When choosing an individual action, determine what you will do and share it with the group. When choosing a group action, determine who will take responsibility for different aspects of the action. The following are secondary suggestions:

1. Determine a specific way in which you will be more responsive to God's promptings.

2. Read at least one parable from the gospels every day this week. Try to understand its meaning in your life. Make a note of your thoughts.

3. The parables are vivid pictures. Draw pictures to illustrate some of these parables. Include your children, family, or friends.

4. If possible, meditate on the parable of the sower and the seeds as you work in your garden. If not, do the same while planting seeds indoors.

5. Write a parable to be shared with the group that expresses a deep feeling or need and that contains a lesson to be learned.

Invitation to Closing Prayer

Give thanks to God (aloud or silently) for insights gained, for desires awakened, for directions clarified, for the gift of one another's openness and sensitivity. Conclude with the following:

Loving Father,
our lives are full of rocky patches and briars.
Many of these obstacles we ourselves create,
for our desires are not rooted in your Word.
Help us renew our love and understanding of your message.

Spirit of God,
be with us and take away our fears.
Strengthen our resolve to nurture the seed
you have planted within us.
Keep us on the right path
where we can grow and truly be your disciples.

Lord Jesus, open our minds,
our eyes, our ears, and our hearts
to your loving presence in our lives.

Amen

SIXTEENTH SUNDAY IN ORDINARY TIME

Three Parables about the Kingdom of God

Invitation to Pray
Pause for a few moments of silence and enter more deeply into the presence of God.

> *Song:* "The Kingdom of God," Bryn Rees

> *Proclaim the gospel:* Matthew 13:24-43
> God's Reign

Take a few minutes to savour a word, a phrase, a question, or a feeling that rises up in you. Reflect on this quietly or share it aloud.

Invitation to Reflect
These parables in Matthew's Gospel focus on the Kingdom of God. Each offers us a dimension of God's reign. God's Kingdom, we believe, will exist in its fullness at the end of the world. God alone will bring it about.

God's Kingdom also exists on earth, although not yet completely fulfilled. We are God's instruments on earth, with Jesus whose Spirit enables us to do God's work. In the Lord's Prayer that Jesus taught us, we pray, "your kingdom come, your will be done, on earth as in heaven".

When Jesus speaks of the tiny mustard seed growing into the huge shrub, he is telling us that God's Kingdom is here. This same thought is true when we are asked to imagine the small amount of yeast that enables the whole mass of dough to rise. Like tiny seeds and small bits of yeast, the Kingdom of God comes into being and gains strength and prominence. The reign of God exists where people treat each other with justice, as Jesus treated all people.

If we value God's people, regardless of their appearance, social stature, or accomplishments, we are acting with justice. The Kingdom of God is furthered when anyone performs deeds of justice. We either nurture its growth or we impede its progress.

Another perspective of God's reign is offered through the parable of the darnel (weeds). Here wheat and weeds grow together until harvest, and then are completely separated. Jesus explains the strong symbolism of this parable. The field is the world; the good seed, those who want to be part of God's kingdom; the darnel, those who choose to follow evil ways. The harvest is the end of the world. Jesus uses very vivid, ancient imagery to explain to his disciples how people will either enter into God's ultimate reign, or through their sinful choices, will be separated from it and receive punishment.

Certainly Jesus was urging his followers to be people of the Kingdom. Rarely does our Lord use such strong language to present his message. In our modern world we do not often consider apostasy, "the fiery furnace," or "wailing and grinding of teeth" (v. 42). However one imagines the end of the world, no believer wants to be separated from God.

Invitation to Group Sharing

1. How have I taken opportunities to be like yeast in a mass of dough?

2. Share an instance when you failed to act justly and did not respect the value of another person.

3. Reflect upon how you picture the final reign of God. Where do I/we see glimpses of God's reign in our world?

4. How can our community be yeast in our parish, neighbourhood, workplace? What will we do to be yeast?

Invitation to Act

Determine a specific action (individual or group) that flows from your sharing. This should be your primary consideration. When choosing an individual action, determine what you will do and share it with the group. When choosing a group action, determine who will take responsibility for different aspects of the action. The following are secondary suggestions:

1. This week perform a tangible act of kindness for someone whom you have not always valued or treated justly.

2. Determine to carry out a specific act of justice.

3. Speak to a few people about their images of God's Kingdom and their own eternal life.

4. Pray daily asking God to show you how you can be a tiny seed of love and justice.

5. Be grateful for those who have nurtured you in any way. If possible, thank the person(s) directly.

Invitation to Closing Prayer
Give thanks to God (aloud or silently) for insights gained, for desires awakened, for directions clarified, for the gift of one another's openness and sensitivity. Conclude with the following:

Leader: For the times we have heard your call and responded with justice,

All: Your kingdom come.

Leader: For the times we have realised our injustices and changed our hearts,

All: Your kingdom come.

Leader: For the times people have loved us even though we were ungrateful and even sinful,

All: Your kingdom come.

Leader: For the times we have been yeast or good seed for others,

All: Your kingdom come.

All: God of Love, Lord of Justice, Spirit of Understanding, we thank you for the blessing of coming together to pray and live in your kingdom.
            Help us to seek your will and your kingdom forever.
            Amen

Close by joining hands and reflectively praying the Lord's Prayer.

Seventeenth Sunday in Ordinary Time

We Treasure the Kingdom of God

Invitation to Pray
Pause for a few moments of silence and enter more deeply into the presence of God.

> *Song:* "Bring Forth the Kingdom," Marty Haugen

> *Proclaim the gospel:* Matthew 13:44-52
> What is the Kingdom of Heaven Like?

Take a few minutes to savour a word, a phrase, a question, or a feeling that rises up in you. Reflect on this quietly or share it aloud.

Invitation to Reflect
In this series of sayings, Jesus continues his teaching about the Kingdom of God. What will it be like? What can we expect? His teaching is both clear as a bell and yet filled with mystery we cannot fully comprehend.

The treasure in the field he describes must have been a very great treasure. The fellow who found it, the text tells us, hid it so he could go and buy the entire field! He sold all he had to possess this great treasure.

And the merchant who sold everything to buy that fine pearl must nearly have put himself out of business. Apparently it wasn't the enterprise of selling pearls that attracted him, but the beauty of the one fine pearl that superseded all others. Half measures won't do when it comes to fine pearls.

And then there is that fishing crew who netted fish of every kind. Here Jesus presents a warning. At the end, only the good fish will be kept; the bad ones will be thrown out and forgotten. Which are the good and which the bad? The text leaves that unclear for us.

In today's world, it can be very difficult to sort out the good pearls or the best fish from all the others. We are confused by a cacophony of noise coming from everywhere: media, World Wide Web, neighbours, family, and our own inner voices. Which voice is of God? How can we sort it out? The key to all this is found in a simple word, easy to overlook, in the first line of the reading. Look again.

Jesus teaches us that the mark of the right choice, the way we can know it, is that we will experience *joy*. In the old Penny Catechism, widely used in the Church until Vatican II, we were taught that God made us to know, love, and serve him, but with the ultimate goal of *being happy*. When you pause to take the temperature of your conscience, finding deep joy tells you that you have made the right choices, even if the times are tough, even if the work is terribly hard. Still, if there is joy deep in your heart, it is a sign that God's reign is present within you.

Invitation to Group Sharing

1. What are the times or decisions in my life that have clearly resulted in a deep inner sense of joy?

2. How could I reflect more fully on the decisions I make to determine if they will lead me to the reign of God?

3. What guidance could Church leadership or members of the Church offer me or the whole community to live more in expectation of the reign of God being realized in everyday life?

Invitation to Act

Determine a specific action (individual or group) that flows from your sharing. This should be your primary consideration. When choosing an individual action, determine what you will do and share it with the group. When choosing a group action, determine who will take responsibility for different aspects of the action. The following are secondary suggestions:

1. At home, talk together at the dinner table about how God's Kingdom is present in your household. In other words, does your daily life lead the members of your household to deep joy and a sense of God's presence?

2. On your own, keep a log of all the decisions you are asked to make in a single week—and your response to each. Don't leave anything out—financial, medical, social, relationships, ministerial, ethical—include everything. Share this with a friend or spiritual director.

3. As a group, establish a network through which people facing difficult choices in your parish can find support and help.

4. Share your joy in belonging to God with someone.

5. Reflect on the blessings in your life. Take time to thank God for them.

Invitation to Closing Prayer

Give thanks to God (aloud or silently) for insights gained, for desires awakened, for directions clarified, for the gift of one another's openness and sensitivity. Conclude with the following:

O Divine Teacher,
> open our ears to hear your voice
> and our eyes to see your presence in our world.

Guide us to choose well
> from the many good avenues
> that are open to each of us.

Send your Spirit to fill us with the fire of love
> and the joy of knowing you are near.

Amen

Eighteenth Sunday in Ordinary Time

"Give Them Some Food Yourselves...."

Invitation to Pray
Pause for a few moments of silence and enter more deeply into the presence of God.

>   ***Song:*** "Love Divine, All Loves Excelling," Charles Wesley

>   ***Proclaim the gospel:*** Matthew 14:13-21
>   The Nourishment of Thousands

Take a few minutes to savour a word, a phrase, a question, or a feeling that rises up in you. Reflect on this quietly or share it aloud.

Invitation to Reflect
How much would it take to feed all the hungry people? This is a question with two answers.

First, not much at all. The Eucharist—the presence of Jesus among us—is all we need to be fully nourished and satisfied. It is the "source and summit of the Christian life" (*Lumen gentium* (document of the Second Vatican Council)). The Eucharist is the single most important and powerful act a believer can undertake. It is really our identity, our assembly, our life.

We could take away all the Church's schools, all the youth centres, all the convents and presbyteries, every parish activity—but if we still have the Eucharist, we're still Catholic. If we filled our schools to the windows and our churches to the rafters, if we had all the buildings and money we thought we'd ever need, if we paved all the parking lots—but didn't have the Eucharist—what would we be? Hungry, starving, and spiritually malnourished.

How much would it take to feed the hungry people? The second answer, which is connected to the first, is that it would take everything we've got. When his disciples asked Jesus this question, his answer was disarming. "Give them some food yourselves" (v. 16), he told them. Yes, you—sitting there reading this. *You.* Jesus was talking about the real bread of everyday nourishment. The real fish needed for dinner tonight.

In today's world, who will feed the hungry? Those nourished with Christ at the Eucharist, that's who. We tend to think the government will do it; or that someone else will surely step in before they starve. But the fact of the matter is that each time we receive Communion, we are receiving the Body of Christ which is also who we are, the *body* of Christ in today's world. Those who are hungry are waiting for us to get moving.

Invitation to Group Sharing

1. How am I nourished spiritually and emotionally? What can I do to provide such nourishment for those I love?

2. How are we, as Christians, particularly called upon to feed those who are hungry? How does this Sunday's gospel help me to answer this question?

3. What resolution can we make now that will help us respond more fully to those around us waiting to be fed?

Invitation to Act

Determine a specific action (individual or group) that flows from your sharing. This should be your primary consideration. When choosing an individual action, determine what you will do and share it with the group. When choosing a group action, determine who will take responsibility for different aspects of the action. The following are secondary suggestions:

1. The next time you receive Communion spend some time reflecting on the real presence of Christ and how we are the Body of Christ.

2. On your own, review your recent credit card statements and cheque book entries and see what story this tells about your own financial decisions relative to those who are poor. Formulate a support system that would enable you to handle personal finances in such a way that the demands of the gospel are met.

3. Organise a parish programme or workshop that helps people reflect how their budget reflects their values. Make this event both an educational and an outreach programme.

4. Reflect on a time when you were nourished—physically, emotionally, spiritually. Express your gratitude for this gift.

5. Be especially attentive during the consecration and Communion at next Sunday's Mass.

Invitation to Closing Prayer

Give thanks to God (aloud or silently) for insights gained, for desires awakened, for directions clarified, for the gift of one another's openness and sensitivity. Conclude with the following:

Jesus, Lord and Provider,
　　we have so much to be thankful for,
　　so much to live on and make us comfortable.
Thank you for calling us to discomfort,
　　to a more generous giving of our time, talent, and treasure.
Thank you for leading us to your reign
　　through the eye of the needle.
Amen

NINETEENTH SUNDAY IN ORDINARY TIME

Be Not Afraid

Invitation to Pray
Pause for a few moments of silence and enter more deeply into the presence of God.

> ***Song:*** "Be Not Afraid," Robert J. Dufford, SJ

> ***Proclaim the gospel:*** Matthew 14:22-33
> The Storm at Sea

Take a few minutes to savour a word, a phrase, a question, or a feeling that rises up in you. Reflect on this quietly or share it aloud.

Invitation to Reflect
In this story, Jesus is responding to a part of the human condition that everyone experiences during storms. Who hasn't found themselves at a time in life when the storm winds seem to blow against their plans, hopes, and dreams? Who hasn't felt just a bit seasick as life tipped first this way, and then that?

But here's a dimension of the story you might overlook: the ministry of Jesus in this situation was not to himself. It was to others. We often read this story and pause to think of *our own storms*, the times or moments in our own lives when everything seemed topsy-turvy. Not so for Jesus.

Jesus knew his disciples. He knew their fears, confusion, losses, moments of despair, desires for love and grace. In calling Peter to come to him upon the water, Jesus was teaching us how to respond to one another. We are to become more aware of one another's fears and needs—and then invite one another to a safe, loving place with us. We are to be Jesus for them.

In today's world, it is easy to imagine people living in stormy times; poor women raising children, abandoned by their husbands; families who have lost their source of income; older adults feeling the first signs of memory loss and confusion; young people with AIDS/HIV; people losing faith; whole nations suffering civil war; children shooting other children; drugs; pornography; abuse; violence; loss of love, and the end of relationships.

Having faith in Jesus, which this narrative leads us to examine, is not mere lip service. It leads us to do what Jesus did: in this case, to call others to the safety and love of relationship *with us* in Christ's name.

Invitation to Group Sharing

1. In the parish where I live, what storms are people enduring of which I am aware? Also, imagine the storms of which you are unaware.

2. What gifts have I received in my own life that would allow me to "be Jesus" in these stormy times and call others to love and safety?

3. What obstacles do I or we face in helping people to safety?

4. How could the parish provide a safer haven for those experiencing stormy times? What can we, as a group, do to help provide this haven?

Invitation to Act

Determine a specific action (individual or group) that flows from your sharing. This should be your primary consideration. When choosing an individual action, determine what you will do and share it with the group. When choosing a group action, determine who will take responsibility for different aspects of the action. The following are secondary suggestions:

1. Think about your own family or circle of close friends. How could you help those who are currently enduring stormy seas?

2. Set up or support a Credit Union in your parish in which those with means can assist those in troubled times with interest-free loans or grants.

3. Together, choose one group in the parish or community most in need of greater safety or security and publicly offer it to them.

4. The next time you find yourself in stormy times, remember to be with the Lord in prayer and to rely on his loving care.

5. Take some time this week to remember and to pray for those who have helped you in stormy times.

Invitation to Closing Prayer

Give thanks to God (aloud or silently) for insights gained, for desires awakened, for directions clarified, for the gift of one another's openness and sensitivity. Conclude with the following:

Loving God,
> open our mind's eye to understand more fully
> what having faith in you leads us to do.
Guide our faltering faith,
> and increase our trust
> so that, like you, we may offer to others
>>   the security,
>>   love,
>>   and wonder of life in you.
Amen

TWENTIETH SUNDAY IN ORDINARY TIME

Your Faith Has Saved You

Invitation to Pray
Pause for a few moments of silence and enter more deeply into the presence of God.

> ***Song:*** "Gather Us In," Marty Haugen

> ***Proclaim the gospel:*** Matthew 15:21-28
> The Faith of the Canaanite Woman

Take a few minutes to savour a word, a phrase, a question, or a feeling that rises up in you. Reflect on this quietly or share it aloud.

Invitation to Reflect
It had been a busy time in Galilee for Jesus and his disciples. After John the Baptist was killed, Jesus withdrew, only to find crowds needing nourishment, and he fed more than five thousand people! Crossing the lake once again, he stilled the stormy seas and called Peter to follow him in faith. Then he healed many who were sick in Gennesaret before encountering yet another argument with some scribes and Pharisees over the interpretation of the law.

Now he had withdrawn to the far side of the lake, where the cities of Tyre and Sidon are found, most likely hoping to rest a little. Here, too, the demands of his ministry prevailed upon him.

He meets a most interesting woman! She was alone in a man's world, a Gentile no less, and she worried about her daughter who was tormented by a demon. She would not leave Jesus alone. His disciples tried to send her away, but she would not leave. In her argument with Jesus, *she calls him to a new attitude* and, most amazingly, he relents and agrees to heal her daughter. No other person in all of Matthew merits Jesus' remark about "such great faith."

In today's Church, it is easy to develop the attitude that what we have is for ourselves, and only for those who are within our boundaries. Like Jesus, we might say that we are sent only to such and such a group, or to people who behave in this or that manner. But in this gospel, we are stretched to

151

new horizons. There are many people knocking on our church doors *whose faith is also great* like this Canaanite woman's. Will we let them in as Jesus did?

Invitation to Group Sharing

1. When have I been welcomed despite appearing to be an outsider, not deserving of the love or forgiveness I was offered?

2. How could we, as a community, respond in a more Christlike manner to those who are divorced, other Christians, gay or lesbian people, newcomers, immigrants, or others?

3. How does our parish make itself a welcoming community? What do I do to be a welcoming presence?

Invitation to Act

Determine a specific action (individual or group) that flows from your sharing. This should be your primary consideration. When choosing an individual action, determine what you will do and share it with the group. When choosing a group action, determine who will take responsibility for different aspects of the action. The following are secondary suggestions:

1. Be a welcoming presence to someone in your family, neighbourhood, or work environment.

2. Pray for those involved in healing: doctors, nurses, psychologists, social workers, spiritual directors. Thank God for their presence and action in helping others.

3. Set up a welcoming group in your parish who would go to unconventional places to reach out to those who feel alienated or rejected. Welcome them back.

4. Consciously choose to move beyond yourself today and be a welcoming, healing presence to someone who is lonely, in prison, or on society's fringes.

Invitation to Closing Prayer

Give thanks to God (aloud or silently) for insights gained, for desires awakened, for directions clarified, for the gift of one another's openness and sensitivity. Conclude with the following:

Jesus, Lord and Giver of Life,
    grant us the courage to love those
    whom you love,
        to seek out the rejected,
        the alienated,
        and the outsider.
Fill our hearts with the fire of your divine love
    and soften our stony hearts
    so that the world may know through us
        that you love everyone.
Amen

Twenty-First Sunday in Ordinary Time

A Powerful Question

Invitation to Pray
Pause for a few moments of silence and enter more deeply into the presence of God.

Song: "Taste and See," Stephen Dean

Proclaim the gospel: Matthew 16:13-20
Who Do You Say I Am?

Take a few minutes to savour a word, a phrase, a question, or a feeling that rises up in you. Reflect on this quietly or share it aloud.

Invitation to Reflect
The disciples were on the road to Caesarea Philippi when Jesus, in the midst of his busiest period of ministry, had something on his mind. This is the heart of the Gospel of Matthew. In just a few verses, the text will begin moving us toward Jerusalem and the Passion. But now Jesus was thinking about a more personal matter.

"Who do people say that the Son of Man is?" (v. 13) he asked them. "What are people saying about *me*?"

It is one of the most searching questions in all of Scripture. It seems to come from the heart of a person at once aware of his destiny and yet still clarifying his mission for his disciples. Certainly all the activity in the previous weeks and months had made them wonder. They were surprised as they saw the crowds gather almost daily, and as they realised how the healing unfolded from his hands.

"But who do *you* say that I am?" (v. 15, emphasis added) he asked. It is a troubling and powerful question. Perhaps it is one that we ourselves might ask a trusted friend about our own "public" lives. "What are people saying about me?" Maybe even famous people would ask this? Even Mother Teresa might have asked this. Maybe Oscar Romero, maybe Martin Luther King?

His apostles venture an answer, "Some say John the Baptist, others Elijah" (v. 14). They didn't mention what still others were saying: madman, fiend, friend of Satan, lawbreaker, or most threatening of all, blasphemer.

His disciples must have wondered, too. "Who is this?" they must have asked among themselves. "How did we get mixed up in this?" Peter then stepped forward, representing us all. "You are the Christ, the Son of the living God" (v. 16), he said, "the one for whom we have been waiting." Little did Peter know how this profession of faith would change his life.

Invitation to Group Sharing
1. Who does the Church say Jesus was and is?

2. How do I experience the presence of Christ in my own life?

3. What does faith in Jesus mean in terms of how I live? In what ways could my faith in Jesus impact more powerfully on my life?

4. In what ways do we, as a parish, not live up to what Jesus would expect from us as his apostles and disciples? What can we do about it? In what ways do we measure up well?

Invitation to Act
Determine a specific action (individual or group) that flows from your sharing. This should be your primary consideration. When choosing an individual action, determine what you will do and share it with the group. When choosing a group action, determine who will take responsibility for different aspects of the action. The following are secondary suggestions:

1. As a group, identify a local group of people to whom Jesus would have responded with love and healing. Pray for them, and if possible, invite them into your parish and your life.

2. This week, pause once each day to become aware of the presence of the risen Christ. Allow this energy to surround you with love.

3. Jesus gave us the key to happiness when he taught us how to live. Choose one of the following actions and practice it this week as your way to happiness: (1) Choose one of your enemies and try to be reconciled with them; (2) Give away a substantial amount of your money; or (3) Speak out in defence of justice.

4. Bring to prayer those who have been a support to you. If possible, thank them personally.

Invitation to Closing Prayer

Give thanks to God (aloud or silently) for insights gained, for desires awakened, for directions clarified, for the gift of one another's openness and sensitivity. Conclude with the following:

Jesus, Lord and Giver of Life,
    we turn to you in faith
    and we proclaim that you are Christ,
        the Messiah!
Fill us with the desire to live according to our beliefs
    and send your Spirit to give us courage,
        strength,
        and purity of heart.
Bind us together for this journey.
Amen

TWENTY-SECOND SUNDAY IN ORDINARY TIME

The Cross and True Happiness

Invitation to Pray
Pause for a few moments of silence and enter more deeply into the presence of God.

> *Song:* "Will You Come and Follow Me," John Bell / Graham Maule

> *Proclaim the gospel:* Matthew 16:21-27
> Self-denial and the Cross

Take a few minutes to savour a word, a phrase, a question, or a feeling that rises up in you. Reflect on this quietly or share it aloud.

Invitation to Reflect
Everyone wants to be happy, right? The deep human desire for happiness and contentment is at the basis of most advertising, most recreational businesses, and many of the decisions we make every day. Everyone wants it.

So why would Jesus teach that we must take up our cross? As it is used in this text, that phrase is *not* a reference to Christ's own eventual death. Crucifixion was a common punishment in the first century Middle East. The cross was a metaphor for suffering and agony. But what is Jesus saying here? How can he be serious?

This is one of those times when Jesus is giving us a "secret" to the kingdom of God. Here is where the contrast between the commercial culture of every age and the teachings of Jesus come into direct conflict. Learning this and living by Jesus' teachings rather than those of our culture will indeed lead to happiness. Our culture is focused more directly upon the gratification of all our desires while the gospels show us how to value our lives in relation to God and to one another.

The self-denial of which Jesus speaks means submitting our own will to God. It means becoming precisely who God intends us to be, nothing more and nothing less. It means living in grace—allowing God's shaping power to form us. When the text speaks of denying ourselves, it means we are to deny that part of ourselves that leads us to sin, to be anything other than *who we really are*. Before making that purchase, planning that trip, responding to someone who has hurt me, or any other such activity, ask the fundamental question: Is this really who I am? Is this who God created me to be?

Might Jesus himself not have asked this question on his own way to the cross?

Invitation to Group Sharing

1. What does taking up the cross mean in my life?

2. Where have I experienced God's communication in my own sense of vocation?

3. How can the Church help people hear God's voice in their own lives more clearly amidst the din of contemporary life? What will I do to hear God's voice this week?

Invitation to Act

Determine a specific action (individual or group) that flows from your sharing. This should be your primary consideration. When choosing an individual action, determine what you will do and share it with the group. When choosing a group action, determine who will take responsibility for different aspects of the action. The following are secondary suggestions:

1. Take a few moments each day to allow the fundamental question posed in the reflection above (Who am I created to be?) to sink into your consciousness.

2. As a group, listen to some of the youth of your parish community. Invite them to talk about their understanding of hearing God's voice in their lives today.

3. Determine how you will allow God's power to form you in a specific area of your life this week.

4. Ask God for help in accepting a particular cross in your life.

Invitation to Closing Prayer
Give thanks to God (aloud or silently) for insights gained, for desires awakened, for directions clarified, for the gift of one another's openness and sensitivity. Conclude with the following:

O Jesus, we believe in you and we love you.
Guide our hearts
    to hear your voice
    within us.
Guide our feet into your pathways,
    lead us to peace,
    lead us to truth,
    and lead us to happiness
        through your cross.
Amen

Twenty-Third Sunday in Ordinary Time

Where Two or Three Are Gathered in My Name

Invitation to Pray

Pause for a few moments of silence and enter more deeply into the presence of God.

> *Song:* "Gather Us In," Marty Haugen

> *Proclaim the gospel:* Matthew 18:15-20
> Prayer

Take a few minutes to savour a word, a phrase, a question, or a feeling that rises up in you. Reflect on this quietly or share it aloud.

Invitation to Reflect

"Anything goes." In today's society, it might seem that this is sometimes true. Being critical of others is not popular. Indeed there is a pressure to feel that everyone should be allowed to live as he or she sees fit, regardless of the old rules and regulations. It seems like the "contemporary way."

But here we have Jesus suggesting something else. Apparently, not every way of living is acceptable for a faithful Christian. In this text, we have a demonstration of that point at which, we might say, the gospel draws the line. If one sins and remains within the community, the text says, he or she must be confronted and, after due process, if he or she refuses to listen, then excommunication is the proper solution.

It sounds rather harsh, doesn't it? Perhaps it is. But what would the offenses be for which such a harsh treatment is suitable? We must look at the broader gospel to grasp this. There we find, for example, that fully half the moral sayings of Jesus deal with the dangers of money and wealth. Many others deal with the necessity of loving one's enemies, of lending without expecting return, of loving others tenderly, and of examining one's own conscience before admonishing others about their sins.

All of this suggests to us that to live the Christian life today, one must gather with trusted friends in a reasonably small group and examine one's life in terms of the gospel. If we find ourselves or one another lacking, we must gently call ourselves or one another forth in a loving way, in the interest of reconciliation. This includes individuals, but also corporations or govern-ments. If one refuses such honesty and does not amend his or her life, then he or she can no longer be considered a full member of the community. If a corporation or government agency does not, then we must protest and call it back to justice.

Invitation to Group Sharing

1. What will change for me this week? How will I (or we) live this gospel passage more fully?

2. How can we build into the life of our community an opportunity for members to reflect on their way of life?

3. Share about a time when you confronted someone in a spirit of care and reconciliation. Is there someone in my life now who needs my concern in this way? What will I do?

Invitation to Act

Determine a specific action (individual or group) that flows from your sharing. This should be your primary consideration. When choosing an individual action, determine what you will do and share it with the group. When choosing a group action, determine who will take respon-sibility for different aspects of the action. The following are secondary suggestions:

1. Determine a specific issue on which you will be more forthright in professing your faith.

2. As a group, devise a method to reflect honestly how you live in light of the gospel. Act on this.

3. Encourage one ministry group in your parish to spend fifteen or twenty minutes in prayer and faith sharing at its meeting. Offer to be of service.

4. If you find yourself in a position of admonishing someone, do it with care and concern, gentleness and compassion. Remember to ask for the Holy Spirit's guidance.

Invitation to Closing Prayer

Give thanks to God (aloud or silently) for insights gained, for desires awakened, for directions clarified, for the gift of one another's openness and sensitivity. Conclude with the following:

God of the righteous and the sinner,
   heal me where I have sinned
   and lead me to your grace.
Send your Spirit into our community
   and give us right judgment.
Help us to be open and honest
   as we help one another live our Christian lives.
Amen

TWENTY-FOURTH SUNDAY IN ORDINARY TIME

Forgive as God Forgives

Invitation to Pray
Pause for a few moments of silence and enter more deeply into the presence of God.

> *Song:* "Freely, Freely," Carol Owens

> *Proclaim the gospel:* Matthew 18:21-35
> The Unforgiving Servant

Take a few minutes to savour a word, a phrase, a question, or a feeling that rises up in you. Reflect on this quietly or share it aloud.

Invitation to Reflect
The familiar story of the unforgiving servant is actually a commentary on an earlier passage in Matthew's Gospel, the Lord's Prayer in chapter 6. Jesus teaches us to forgive, and goes on in the very next verse to repeat that teaching and underscore it. "If you forgive others," he tells us, "your heavenly Father will forgive you" (Matthew 6:14). But if you don't forgive . . . watch out!

Throughout this gospel, Jesus reveals, little by little, the secrets of the Kingdom of God. There is a teaching on the dangers of wealth; then one on the need to deny oneself; and now this rather mysterious teaching on forgiveness. In each of these teachings, we learn that God is good, generous, and forgiving, and that we must be, too!

This message is not only a secret to the Kingdom of God, but also the secret to a fully happy life. The two become one, you see. If you forgive, Jesus might have said, you will be happy. But if you don't, you will be miserable, dragging around behind you a heavy load of resentment, anger, and hostility.

Many Catholics (as well as people of other faith traditions) grew up believing that if they just followed the laws, they would be saved. But the teachings of Jesus go deeper than that. Will merely following the law be enough to touch your heart and make you forgiving? We must go out of our way to forgive, no matter how large the debt, no matter how often the transgression, no matter how hurt we have been. This gospel seems to suggest that in order to be fully healed and experience the 'salve' of salvation, we must dig deeply into our souls and forgive—no matter what.

And just a few months later, Jesus showed us precisely what this means. On the cross he turned to his killers and forgave them. It is as if he were saying in that act, "Do you think that this, even *this*, can stop me from loving you? Never. I will never stop loving you." Here is true salvation.

Invitation to Group Sharing

1. Do I feel confident enough of God's love in my own life to forgive those around me? Why or why not? If not, how can I become more aware of God's abounding love for me?

2. How have I experienced the generous forgiveness of someone?

3. Whom have I or we not forgiven? Against whom do I feel anger and hostility rather than love and forgiveness?

4. How do we, as a community, forgive those who sin against us? What can we do to foster forgiveness or reconciliation?

Invitation to Act

Determine a specific action (individual or group) that flows from your sharing. This should be your primary consideration. When choosing an individual action, determine what you will do and share it with the group. When choosing a group action, determine who will take responsibility for different aspects of the action. The following are secondary suggestions:

1. In your next period of personal prayer, pray for those whom you hold at a distance and begin the process of forgiving them. Act upon it.

2. As a group, make a list of those whose forgiveness you wish to have. Make another list of those who may be asking your forgiveness. Bring these lists to your prayer.

3. Pray about the need for forgiveness in your own life. Make a commitment to ask for forgiveness from someone you have wronged and/or to offer forgiveness to someone who has hurt you.

4. Make a special effort to be a healing, forgiving presence at home, at work, or at play.

5. Recall instances when you have been forgiven. Thank God and the person(s) for the gift of forgiveness that has freed you.

Invitation to Closing Prayer

Give thanks to God (aloud or silently) for insights gained, for desires awakened, for directions clarified, for the gift of one another's openness and sensitivity. Conclude with the following:

Jesus, you forgave your killers
    even as they nailed you to the cross.
Teach us to forgive,
    to forget ourselves in love,
    to take the tremendous risk of letting go.
Send your Spirit into our lives
    to move our hearts
    and shape our souls
    so that we might forgive those
    who have sinned against us.
Amen

TWENTY-FIFTH SUNDAY IN ORDINARY TIME

The Generosity of God

Invitation to Pray
Pause for a few moments of silence and enter more deeply into the presence of God.

>   ***Song:*** "Praise to the Holiest," John Henry Newman

>   ***Proclaim the gospel:*** Matthew 20:1-16a
>   The Workers in the Vineyard

Take a few minutes to savour a word, a phrase, a question, or a feeling that rises up in you. Reflect on this quietly or share it aloud.

Invitation to Reflect
It is nearly impossible for us to fathom the grace of God. In the first place, it is free and we cannot earn it, no matter how early we show up in the vineyard. Secondly, it is given to *all* who respond to the divine invitation. And what is most amazing about it is that *the same grace* is given to all.

For those who struggle to figure out what God wants and follow it, this is good news indeed. It is not that we are lazy and certainly not that we are heartless. But for some of us, the right moment has not occurred, or the right elements have not fallen into place. We stand on the edge of faith peering in, wondering how those already giving their entire lives to God can do so. What has touched them so deeply that they no longer look back? What has moved them to embrace God's love so fully? Are we open to 'being hired' by God?

In this gospel passage we learn that we, too, will be paid in full. We, too, will be given God's total love, God's totally generous offer of grace. Even when we come rather late to the table, the feast is still plentiful.

The key phrase in this gospel passage may well be the one the workers used in responding to the owner of the vineyard. "Why do you stand here idle all day?" (v. 6) he asked them. "They answered, 'Because no one has hired us'" (v. 7), indicating their willingness and desire to work. Their idleness is not laziness, not indifference, not even a lack of interest. It is that no one has called them, no one has given them work.

166

Perhaps the lesson in this for us is simply that, as long as we desire the work of God's vineyard, as long as we are ready to undertake the labour of love, God is ready to receive and accept us in full. God's grace is so large, and God's love so far-reaching that everyone who responds when called will be treated as an equal daughter or son of God.

Invitation to Group Sharing

1. When have I experienced God's generous love, even though I was slow to respond? To what have I been called that I did not respond?

2. Do I feel confident that God's grace is enough for me? Why or why not? How do I express this confidence?

3. How do we resist God's love, refuse to undertake the labour of love to which God calls us? What can we do to overcome this resistance?

4. How do we, as a community and parish, experience God's grace and love? What more can we do to extend God's grace and love to others?

Invitation to Act

Determine a specific action (individual or group) that flows from your sharing. This should be your primary consideration. When choosing an individual action, determine what you will do and share it with the group. When choosing a group action, determine who will take responsibility for different aspects of the action. The following are secondary suggestions:

1. Commit to praying each day this week for a particular person in need. Maybe you could let the person know you are praying for him or her.

2. Many people do not respond to the work of the reign of God because they do not know it is there to be done. Formulate a list of opportunities (feeding those who are hungry, visiting those who are sick or lonely, working in the peace or justice movement, teaching the young, seeking rights for homeless people, orphans, immigrants, or those who are rejected) and make it public in the parish. Decide on one such activity that you, as an individual or as a group, will support or undertake.

3. Act generously and lovingly toward someone in your family, a friend, a colleague, a neighbour, or a stranger.

4. Count your blessings, especially the many ways God is generous to you.

Invitation to Closing Prayer

Give thanks to God (aloud or silently) for insights gained, for desires awakened, for directions clarified, for the gift of one another's openness and sensitivity. Conclude with the following:

O God, whose generous love we receive,
    create in us hearts ready for your vineyard,
    and hands able to work for you.
Guide us to understand your call,
    to desire your will,
    and to go to work when you invite us.
Send your Spirit into our lives
    to make us loving women and men,
    so your reign will be established
    on earth as in heaven.
Amen

TWENTY-SIXTH SUNDAY IN ORDINARY TIME

Doing What We Say We Will

Invitation to Pray
Pause for a few moments of silence and enter more deeply into the presence of God.

> *Song:* "At the Name of Jesus," Caroline Maria Noel
> *Proclaim the gospel:* Matthew 21:28-32
> The Story of Two Sons

Take a few minutes to savour a word, a phrase, a question, or a feeling that rises up in you. Reflect on this quietly or share it aloud.

Invitation to Reflect
This story is not about two sons. It is about two kinds of religious people—those who appear faithless, but in the end follow the law written upon their hearts by God, and those who claim to be faithful, but do not actually *live* according to their beliefs. For Matthew, faith is never enough in and of itself. It must always be translated into a *lifestyle*. It must be lived. It must result in the establishment of God's reign within and among us.

Matthew shocks his audience a little here. Tax collectors and prostitutes, he tells this crowd of religious insiders, are entering the Kingdom of God before them. To us the message is the same: those outside your church who seem least likely may be hearing God's Word in their hearts. They may be living lives of love and gentleness, generosity and forgiveness, prayer and desire for God. They may enter the Kingdom of God before you.

Over and over again in Matthew we learn that the reign of God is not what we expect it to be. How blind we are! How difficult for us to see!

This story presents a son who first said, "No!" when his father asked him to work in the vineyard. All along he knew he needed to repent. He knew he did not love perfectly enough. Perhaps his own imperfections were his salvation. Those who believe they are righteous, those who believe they are worthy of the gifts of grace, watch out! Their sense of self-righteousness may lead them to reject the very compassion and love they seek in God's reign. They say "Yes," with their lips, but their heart is not loving.

Most of us live on both sides of this parable. Sometimes we say, "no," but mean "yes," and other times we say "yes," but then never go.

Invitation to Group Sharing

1. Do I believe I am faithful enough? Why? How do I express my faithfulness?

2. How have I experienced both sides of this parable in my own life?

3. How can we become more faithful in word *and* in deed?

Invitation to Act

Determine a specific action (individual or group) that flows from your sharing. This should be your primary consideration. When choosing an individual action, determine what you will do and share it with the group. When choosing a group action, determine who will take responsibility for different aspects of the action. The following are secondary suggestions:

1. As an individual or as a group, brainstorm a list of ways you could be more faithful in deed to God's Word. Determine a specific action around one of these.

2. Develop a method in which you, as a group, can witness to your larger parish community, calling the people to a more faithful response in a specific area of need.

3. Invite some faithful people who are also "religious outsiders" into your next meeting. Talk with them about how they are faithful to their conscience, the law written in their hearts by God.

4. Be patient with those who change their minds. Try to meet them where they are.

Invitation to Closing Prayer

Give thanks to God (aloud or silently) for insights gained, for desires awakened, for directions clarified, for the gift of one another's openness and sensitivity. Conclude with the following:

We come before you now,
    O good and holy God and Father,
    and pray for faith.
Help us believe
    and live by what we profess.
Open our hearts to those around us
    who are signs of fidelity to you.
Help us live
    by radical faith.
Let your Spirit fill us with love
      and your Son fill us with faith.
Amen

TWENTY-SEVENTH SUNDAY IN ORDINARY TIME

God Deals Fairly with Us

Invitation to Pray
Pause for a few moments of silence and enter more deeply into the presence of God.

> *Song:* "Lord of All Hopefulness," Jan Struther

> *Proclaim the gospel:* Matthew 21:33-43
> The Wicked Tenants

Take a few minutes to savour a word, a phrase, a question, or a feeling that rises up in you. Reflect on this quietly or share it aloud.

Invitation to Reflect
Here we have a marvellous gospel story that, in itself, leads us to understand more deeply the message of Jesus. How will God deal with us? What can we expect? This story gives us a rather stark portrayal.

In verse 34, the text tells us that the harvest was near, literally, 'the time of fruit.' This suggests to us that, in the Christian life, time is always of the essence. It is always urgent for us to be about the reign of God. The vineyard of which this story speaks, of course, is that very reign.

The allegory here is clear. God has given us this vineyard—and all the tools we need to tend it. The harvest is upon us. Prophets were sent to call us home, but we did not listen to them. But God, faithful to the end, did not give up. Instead, he sent his very own Son. Surely we would listen to him, God thought. But him we also rejected.

This is a story about the leaders of God's Chosen People; it is also a story about us. Indeed, the time of the harvest is near. The work of the Kingdom of God falls upon us—and we have all the tools we need to do what God wants. But will we listen to those who speak for God, our modern prophets? Or will we reject them, greedily hoping to have the vineyard to ourselves?

The point is not merely a matter of running a good vineyard. The wicked tenants did that, after all. It is a matter of producing fruit for God that is the central issue here, rather than seeking our own selfish interests. It is easy for us to confuse this.

What does God want? God wants:
respect for all life (see John 10:10, Psalm 139:13-18, Matthew 5:21-24);
forgiveness (see Matthew 18:21, 22, Luke 17:3, 4, John 20:23);
mercy (see Matthew 9:13, Matthew 12:7, Luke 10:36, 37);
for the poor to be fed, the ill nursed, the lonely visited, the imprisoned set free (see Matthew 25:37-40);
for us to be generous (see 1 Timothy 6:18);
to love our enemies (see Matthew 5:44, Luke 6:27, 35);
to take care of the poor (see Isaiah 58:7).

Reading Scripture as a whole, we can plainly see what God wants.

Invitation to Group Sharing

1. Do I have an inner sense of what God wants for the unborn, for those oppressed, or the imprisoned? Of how God wants me to treat these people?

2. When have I been ministered to by other Christians?

3. How have we, as a community, witnessed God's response to our real needs?

4. What work remains if God's Kingdom is to be established in our corner of the world?

Invitation to Act

Determine a specific action (individual or group) that flows from your sharing. This should be your primary consideration. When choosing an individual action, determine what you will do and share it with the group. When choosing a group action, determine who will take responsibility for different aspects of the action. The following are secondary suggestions:

1. Read through the Gospel of Matthew from front to back and make a list of different gospel values. Include everything. In your prayer each day, ask the Spirit to help you live one aspect of this gospel value lifestyle.

2. Take a concrete step this week to embrace the gospel of life. Find out about the organisations that promote Life issues, (eg.

173

SPUC and Life). Are there any local meetings in your area? Think about attending one.

3. Familiarise yourself with the Church's teachings on life issues. Begin with the *Gospel of Life* (Pope John Paul II) and *Cherishing Life* (Catholic Bishops' Conference of England & Wales, 2004).

4. Take ten minutes each day this week for time alone with God. How are the qualities of the Kingdom reflected in your life?

Invitation to Closing Prayer

Give thanks to God (aloud or silently) for insights gained, for desires awakened, for directions clarified, for the gift of one another's openness and sensitivity. Conclude with the following:

Choose one person to read Psalm 139:13-16. Invite each participant to share a word or a phrase from the psalm that speaks to his or her heart.

Leader: Jesus, Lord and Giver of Life,
we share our faith in you with each other
All: and believe that you are the Son of God.
Leader: Help us hear the prophets you send us
and let us be changed
by their witness.
All: And help us love you more faithfully
especially in recognising your Father's eyes in those
who are unborn, infirm, imprisoned or abused.
Amen

TWENTY-EIGHTH SUNDAY IN ORDINARY TIME

The Wedding Feast

Invitation to Pray
Pause for a few moments of silence and enter more deeply into the presence of God.

> ***Song:*** "Gather Us In," Marty Haugen

> ***Proclaim the gospel:*** Matthew 22:1-14
> The Heavenly Banquet

Take a few minutes to savour a word, a phrase, a question, or a feeling that rises up in you. Reflect on this quietly or share it aloud.

Invitation to Reflect
Over and over again in the Gospel of Matthew, we are given a warning. Even though the Kingdom of God is meant to include us, if we do not shape up and embrace the message of Jesus, we will be dropped from the guest list.

God is not obliged to invite us. The invitation is pure graciousness on God's part. And who knows how that invitation will appear? It could be in the form of a person with a terminal illness, inviting us to a new level of compassion and acceptance. It could be in the form of a displaced person, calling us to open our arms to embrace him or her. It could be in the form of a family lost in the travail of homelessness, joblessness, chemical dependency, abuse, violence, or lost love. It could be someone right within our family.

Who is calling you? This text from Matthew makes it clear that, indeed, the king has sent servants to summon you. By baptism you have been initiated, and are a member of the Church. But now the burden is on you to listen to the king's servants, to respond to their call, and to come to the feast. Now is the time to join the celebration!

Do not make excuses. "I haven't time—I've bought a cow." "I can't come—I'm getting married." "Sorry—I'm working on my Web site." Do not come without that baptismal garment, the garment of Christ—forgiveness, respect for life, tenderness, love, mercy, and kindness. If you only give lip service to the king, you will be thrown out on your ear.

Don't forget the feast is for the "bad and good alike." Re-read verse 10 several times. Let its message sink in deeply. The mystery of the Kingdom of God unfolds for us like a flower, petal by petal. God, it seems, is more concerned with having a great party than sorting out the bad from the good here.

Invitation to Group Sharing

1. How do I hear God's invitation to the wedding feast? Who is calling and inviting me? How will I respond?

2. Whom have I called? How do I invite others through my faith response?

3. How does my parish community welcome the good as well as the "not-so-good" to the feast? Is anyone not welcome? Why?

4. How can we, as a community, echo the teaching of Jesus in this parable?

Invitation to Act

Determine a specific action (individual or group) that flows from your sharing. This should be your primary consideration. When choosing an individual action, determine what you will do and share it with the group. When choosing a group action, determine who will take responsibility for different aspects of the action. The following are secondary suggestions:

1. Organise a meal and invite unlikely guests to join you. Later, reflect on this as an expression of the reign of God.

2. This week be a welcoming presence to those with whom you live, work, or play.

3. If someone prepares a meal for you, show your appreciation.

Invitation to Closing Prayer

Give thanks to God (aloud or silently) for insights gained, for desires awakened, for directions clarified, for the gift of one another's openness and sensitivity. Conclude with the following:

O God, the Giver of Feasts,
> thank you for inviting us to your banquet
> and for welcoming us as we are.
Create in our hearts the same compassion,
> the same trusting love,
> so we will welcome those
> society rejects.
Send your Holy Spirit to mold us
> and inspire us to fill the hall with your guests
> so we will hold a great party in your name.
Amen

Twenty-Ninth Sunday in Ordinary Time

Discipleship and Politics

Invitation to Pray
Pause for a few moments of silence and enter more deeply into the presence of God.

> *Song:* "Sing a New Song," Daniel L. Schutte, SJ

> *Proclaim the gospel:* Matthew 22:15-21
> "Is It Lawful...?"

Take a few minutes to savour a word, a phrase, a question, or a feeling that rises up in you. Reflect on this quietly or share it aloud.

Invitation to Reflect
We know this gospel story so well that it is easy to dismiss it as a justification for separating politics from religion. But that would serve to distort and miss the important principle Jesus sets before his followers, both then and now.

Israel was an occupied nation, having been conquered by Rome. As Matthew's Gospel proceeds, there is a growing antagonism between Jesus and the religious and political authorities of his day. In their effort to entrap him, some Herodian sympathisers and some disciples of the Pharisees try to trap Jesus with the highly volatile question of taxes, "Is it lawful to pay the census tax to Caesar or not?" (v. 17). Let us look carefully at Jesus' response. He first asks for a denarius, retorting with another question regarding the image engraved upon the coin. Just the fact that a coin is produced reveals the compromising position of these Jews at the time. No strict Jew would carry a graven image of an emperor, pictured as divine. But the Jews, dominated by Rome, had to tolerate several compromising situations to survive. Thus, the question of taxes being paid to Rome, disdained by the conquered people, has resolved itself. Jesus merely highlights the status quo in both the action of asking for the coin and in his words, "Then repay to Caesar what belongs to Caesar and to God what belongs to God" (v. 21).

This last phrase, "...and to God what belongs to God" (v. 21), contains the core message of Jesus' response to the trickery of his opponents. God's image is deeply engraved upon each human person. God's sovereignty extends over all of creation. Thus, we cannot compartmentalise our lives, separating religion from politics, the spiritual from the worldly. We are whole persons who act out of our gospel values in all areas of life: work, politics, family, parish, and neighbourhood. To separate these spheres of our life is to violate our basic nature. Ultimately, at our core, we are whole persons, created in God's image (see Genesis 1:26, 27), acting out of our religious convictions within an ever-widening circle of influence. All of creation, marked in the image of God and touched by the finger of God, is sacred.

Invitation to Group Sharing

1. When have I felt touched by the finger of God? Where does the Holy Spirit ask me to protect life as sacred today?

2. When have I encountered another, remembering that she or he is created in God's image? How have I witnessed my attitudes and actions change?

3. Where have I noticed a lack of respect for life? What can I do to promote a greater respect for life?

4. What particular injustice to people who are poor or marginalised in our society do I or we feel passionate about? What actions can we take to attempt to change systems of injustice in this area, even in some small way?

Invitation to Act

Determine a specific action (individual or group) that flows from your sharing. This should be your primary consideration. When choosing an individual action, determine what you will do and share it with the group. When choosing a group action, determine who will take responsibility for different aspects of the action. The following are secondary suggestions:

1. Read the newspapers with an eye to detect the deep-rooted injustices in our culture. As a group, discuss what you discover and determine a positive action.
2. Affirm someone who has shown courage in respecting life.

3. Honour the sacredness of the created world by living more lightly on this earth. Together, make a list of ecological practices you

can adopt to reduce waste and avoid the lure of consumerism.

4. Give God praise and thanks that you belong to him.

Invitation to Closing Prayer

Give thanks to God (aloud or silently) for insights gained, for desires awakened, for directions clarified, for the gift of one another's openness and sensitivity. Conclude with the following:

Conclude with the following prayer:

> The earth is yours, O Creator,
>> and all that dwells therein is sacred.
> There is nothing that exists
>> without your mark of divine love.
> Enlighten our minds, open our hearts
>> empower us to act with justice.
> Help us feed the hungry, rather than hoard
>> clothe the impoverished, rather than consume
>> give out of our wants and our needs, rather than oppress.
> We pray that justice will reign on the earth
>> and the light of your *shalom* will break through the darkness.
> We ask this through Jesus and in the Holy Spirit.
> Amen

How Do I Love My Neighbour?

Invitation to Pray
Pause for a few moments of silence and enter more deeply into the presence of God.

> *Song:* "Make Me a Channel of Your Peace," Sebastian Temple

> ***Proclaim the gospel***: Matthew 22:34-40
> The Greatest Commandment

Take a few minutes to savour a word, a phrase, a question, or a feeling that rises up in you. Reflect on this quietly or share it aloud.

Invitation to Reflect
Jesus, confronted by some Pharisees with another question intended to trap him, reveals more insight into living as his follower. In raising this question of the law concerning the greatest commandment, Jesus did not say anything new. Both Deuteronomy 6:5, "You shall love the Lord, your God, with all your heart, and with all your soul, and with all your strength," and Leviticus 19:18, "Take no revenge and cherish no grudge....You shall love your neighbour as yourself," speak of living in love. But few had ever placed these two commandments of love together. In drawing the parallel between love of God and neighbour, Jesus casts a new light upon love of neighbour. The command to love one's neighbour is as imporant as the command to love God.

It is important to notice this revolutionary idea that love of one's neighbour embodies love of God. In Jesus' time, the notion of heavy and light laws prevailed. The love of God was considered in the category of a serious precept, while the love of neighbour was considered less important when there seemed to be a conflict of time or place for observing both. Therefore, once again, Jesus presents a deeper interpretation of the law in his response to another trick question on the part of the religious leaders of his time! When coupled with Jesus' equally provocative notion of who one's neighbours are—"everyone," this second, but equal commandment is even more astounding.

While it is easy to proclaim love for an invisible God with words and pious actions, it is not so simple to love the God presented before us daily in the persons we meet. Love of neighbour is a way to loving God. As we read in the Letter of John (1 John 4:12), "No one has ever seen God. Yet, if we love one another, God remains in us, and his love is brought to perfection in us." Thus the task of the Christian who proclaims to love God is forever transformed.

To love God and our neighbour does not mean that we love only those near us or those who are like us. It also means that we are to love those the world neglects. To love God, one must care for those who are unborn, poor, homeless, and hungry. We must also stretch ourselves to care for those who are unfriendly, those whose manner repels us, those whom we are inclined to dislike. Love of God impels us to treat others with dignity, respect, and honour, including our enemies.

Because God first loved us (see 1 John 4:19), we are gifted with the ability to help those at the margins of society, releasing those imprisoned by addictions, mental illness, and physical limitations. Our gifts are given for the sake of those blinded by prejudice, impoverished by Western material-ism, and sickened by an abusive and violent society. Just as love of God is all-inclusive, love of neighbour encompasses everyone and everything. The covenant that binds us to Christ forever seals us to one another in the God who so loved the world that "...the Word became flesh/ and made his dwelling among us" (John 1:14).

Invitation to Group Sharing

1. How does Jesus' making these two laws of love into one equally important commandment impact on me?

2. Who are some of the 'neighbours' I encounter each day who might be difficult to love?

3. What gifts have we received from our loving God, which can be used to manifest our love for these "neighbours" in our midst?

4. How can we live out this commandment to love God and our neighbour as we love our very self in the real world of our daily lives?

Invitation to Act

Determine a specific action (individual or group) that flows from your sharing. This should be your primary consideration. When choosing an individual action, determine what you will do and share it with the group. When choosing a group action, determine who will take responsibility for different aspects of the action. The following are secondary suggestions:

1. Reach out this week to a carer of the sick or elderly. With a telephone call or letter, affirm his or her role in shepherding those facing suffering or death.

2. Look around your neighbourhood for opportunities to love others by discovering the hidden needs of families nearby. Do the same at work. Listen with a compassionate heart and offer your care in word and deed. Share some of your experiences with others in the group.

3. Together, explore opportunities to work with those who are poor, hungry, single parents, imprisoned or homeless through organised activities already present in your parish. If there are none, plan a way in which to begin a ministry that practices love of neighbour in light of the gospel.

4. Determine your own gifts for loving others by examining your past experiences of crises and struggles. Generally these difficult times are a fountainhead of gifts to help others with similar struggles. As a group, name these gifts and discern concrete ways you can act in love for those in need.

5. Show a family member, a friend or a colleague a sign of love this week.

Invitation to Closing Prayer
Give thanks to God (aloud or silently) for insights gained, for desires awakened, for directions clarified, for the gift of one another's openness and sensitivity. Conclude with the following:

Conclude with the following prayer:

We long to proclaim our love for you,
    O Father,
but mere words are not enough.
Give us the gift of courage to
    live in love with one another
    that in so doing we will truly love you in
        the face of our brothers and sisters.
We are one body in Jesus.
Renew our spirits so we will
    learn to love and care for
Christ's body—
    feeding the hungry
    clothing the naked
    giving drink to the thirsty
    liberating the captives
    embracing the unwanted, unborn, sick, and elderly
    healing the hurts that separate and divide
        us from one another.
    Through the power of your Holy Spirit and in Jesus' name,
    we pray.
Amen

Thirty-First Sunday in Ordinary Time

Integrating Faith and Life

Invitation to Pray
Pause for a few moments of silence and enter more deeply into the presence of God.

> *Song:* "Dear Lord and Father of Mankind," John Greenleaf Whittier

> *Proclaim the gospel:* Matthew 23:1-12
> Practice What You Preach

Take a few minutes to savour a word, a phrase, a question, or a feeling that rises up in you. Reflect on this quietly or share it aloud.

Invitation to Reflect
Care must be taken to avoid reading this passage of Matthew's Gospel without knowing its historical context. It is likely that Matthew's writing of his Gosel was after the destruction of the Jerusalem temple in 70A.D. The evangelist had several issues to deal with in his community of Jews who followed Jesus. Roman occupation at this time was reinforced. Judaism was in a great spiritual and political upheaval and was undergoing consolidation both in authority and orthodoxy. It is easy to understand how the relationship between Jewish authorities of the time and the Christian Jesus movement deteriorated. Thus, Matthew's Gospel, written for his own community, is an attempt to help this emergent Jewish sect of Jesus' followers (not yet called Christians) live the faith in their new circumstances.

It is important to read the harsh critique against the leaders of the larger Jewish community of Matthew's own day in this historical light. Furthermore, it is vital that the reader of today enters into the meaning of the passage and understands that: "We are the Pharisees"—well-intentioned people who struggle to integrate faith and life. We cannot remain spectators to the gospels, for in their timeless revelation, they are about us!

The passage begins by assuring the community of Christian Jews that the way to be faithful to the Law of Moses is to be faithful to the teachings of Jesus, who came to fulfill the Law. For us today, it is an admonition to move beyond the Ten Commandments to ponder and live as Jesus did, particularly as expressed in the Sermon on the Mount. We are instructed to practice what we preach, that is, to avoid the pitfalls of hypocrisy. Lack of compassion, acting unjustly, walking over others to succeed, false piety, and arrogant pride are not part of the vision of Jesus for his followers. Jesus offers an alternative way of life for his community: respect for others, attention to weaker members, compassion for the sinner, and continual forgiveness are the ideals we are to pursue. Leadership in the community does not automatically follow from titles of honour, because all authority comes from God. In Jesus' vision, everyone in the Christian community leads through serving the rest.

Servant leadership; living what we preach; and integrating faith, life, and faithfulness into the way of Jesus set apart the community of Christians. This is the formula for achieving greatness in the Kingdom of God.

Invitation to Group Sharing

1. Reread the gospel passage from Matthew 23:1-12 in light of the context of the early Christian community, placing yourself into the passage. What new insights into my own Christian living do I discover?

2. Reflect upon examples of individuals you have encountered who have integrated faith and life. What characteristics, values, and/or principles seem to guide their daily living?

3. How can we live out the mandate to embrace life from conception to natural death?

4. What are some ways my community can become servant leaders to the wider community?

Invitation to Act

Determine a specific action (individual or group) that flows from your sharing. This should be your primary consideration. When choosing an individual action, determine what you will do and share it with the group. When choosing a group action, determine who will take responsibility for different aspects of the action. The following are secondary suggestions:

1. Determine a specific way to live out your faith this week in an area of life that is difficult.

2. At the Sunday Mass, notice those who seem to be alone, who are

strangers, who look different, or are absent. Make an effort to welcome, to sit with, to open a conversation, or to extend an invitation to these individuals.

3. Learn more about Judaism by inviting a Jewish acquaintance to share his or her faith with your group or by encouraging your parish to sponsor a Jewish-Christian dialogue.

4. Name an area where you find it difficult to integrate your faith. Discuss this with another person. Perhaps you might like to seek guidance on how to live your faith more fully in this circumstance.

5. Act with humility in your endeavours this week.

Invitation to Closing Prayer
Give thanks to God (aloud or silently) for insights gained, for desires awakened, for directions clarified, for the gift of one another's openness and sensitivity. Conclude with the following:

Spirit of the Living God,
    captivate our imagination
    empower our will
    energise our spirit
so we will learn to take our inner convictions
    and live them out more fully day by day.
Jesus, Saviour and companion,
    strengthen our determination
        to follow your way of service
        to open our hearts to forgive
        to embrace searcher, sinner, and saint alike
so we will integrate your way, your truth, and your life
    into our lives.
God our Father and Creator, source of all that is,
    give us grace to live your
        way of love
        as we meet one another
        on this journey of faith.
Blessed be your name. Amen

THIRTY-SECOND SUNDAY IN ORDINARY TIME

God's Plan Is Unfolding

Invitation to Pray
Pause for a few moments of silence and enter more deeply into the presence of God.

> ***Song:*** "O Jesus Christ, Remember," Edward Caswall

> ***Proclaim the gospel:*** Matthew 25:1-13
> Stay Awake

Take a few minutes to savour a word, a phrase, a question, or a feeling that rises up in you. Reflect on this quietly or share it aloud.

Invitation to Reflect
Today's parable of the ten bridesmaids waiting for the groom's arrival is reminiscent of several similar kingdom parables found throughout Matthew's Gospel. The lessons found in the parables of the talents, the separation of the sheep and goats, and the guests invited to the wedding feast all contain lessons about God's unfolding plan—God's reign. The reign of God was made definitive with the birth of Jesus, but is not yet fulfilled. Like the disciples in Jesus' time, we live in the incomplete time between the inception of God's plan for creation and its completion. These parables reveal to us this "in-between-time" is a time for watchfulness and readiness.

To better grasp the implications of this parable, we must first understand the marriage customs in the Judeo-Galilean world of Jesus' day. Whole villages followed the wedding drum to celebrate the nuptials. Bartering between the groom and bride's father could go on for hours, even days. The longer the negotiations, the more the bride was valued and treasured. While the bride, fully arrayed in her wedding dress, stood ready to meet her groom at a moment's notice, several virgins, most likely chosen by the groom, also waited in readiness for the groom's arrival. These women formed a welcoming party at the groom's house or that of his father. The bride would then be brought to the house where a week's feasting and celebrating would occur. It is easy to understand that long waits during the negotiations were part and parcel of the normal wedding preparations. Therefore, to be chosen as part of the groom's welcoming party without proper lamp oil is not only an insult to the bride, but also negligent on the part of the five foolish bridesmaids.

The sudden and unexpected arrival of the groom in this parable is compared to the surprising and spontaneous arrival of God's coming. The bridegroom, Christ, will come again, inviting all to the heavenly banquet. We will either be prepared to meet the Risen One or will have foolishly failed to live in anticipation of this encounter.

But what does this warning of watchful readiness mean for us today? To be prepared to meet Christ in the Kingdom, we must recognise him each day in the persons we encounter. How can we expect to share the heavenly banquet with those we have despised or ignored in this life? Thus, our preparedness for the coming of Christ necessarily involves using our gifts wisely and generously, as well as living out the spiritual and corporal works of mercy.

We make ourselves ready by doing the will of God here and now. The oil of prayer, Scripture, and Eucharist replenishes our lamps in this "in-between" wait. It is foolish to put off cultivating a relationship with God until later in life when we think we will have more time. Instead, each day is an invitation to come to know the God revealed in the Scriptures by reading and pondering their meaning; by spending time in conversation (prayer) with the Lord; and by bringing forth the Kingdom of God in actions that spill over with love. This is the wisdom of readiness, preparation, and anticipation of the coming of God's reign, lest we come to that final encounter and God says to us, "I do not know you!" (v. 13).

Invitation to Group Sharing

1. What is my initial reaction to the message of this parable? How can it influence my daily life?

2. Together, re-read the passage, placing yourselves in the scene: the wise maids with enough oil are half of the group and the foolish maids who are locked out of the feast are the other half. What are some of the insights and feelings you discover as you enter into the parable?

3. What are some practical attitudes and actions that will keep my "oil" of faith, hope, and love replenished?

4. What does the concept of "readiness " or "watchfulness" mean to me, to the group?

Invitation to Act

Determine a specific action (individual or group) that flows from your sharing. This should be your primary consideration. When choosing an individual action, determine what you will do and share it with the group. When choosing a group action, determine who will take responsibility for different aspects of the action. The following are secondary suggestions:

1. Set aside a regular time each day just to talk to God, meditate, write in your journal, or pray with the Scriptures.

2. Further enhance the reign of God by offering your talents to a ministry in the parish or in your community. Soup kitchens, working with the bereaved, catechetical ministries, and visiting the sick and housebound are some of the options.

3. Take the time each night to name, and if you choose, to write down all the encounters you have had during the day. Reflect upon these experiences to discover how Christ was revealed to you in these people.

4. Look over the closing prayer naming the spiritual and corporal works of mercy. Choose to work on one that is most difficult for you.

5. Thank God for those in your life who are wise. If possible, thank them personally.

Invitation to Closing Prayer

Give thanks to God (aloud or silently) for insights gained, for desires awakened, for directions clarified, for the gift of one another's openness and sensitivity. Conclude with the following:

Lord of Life, empower us
    with the guidance of your Spirit to
    live in readiness for your coming in the ways we
        feed the hungry,
        give drink to the thirsty,
        shelter the homeless,
        clothe the naked,
        care for the sick,
        visit prisoners,
        bury the dead,
        share knowledge of you,
        give advice to those in need,
        comfort those who suffer,
        show patience to others,
        forgive one another,
        admonish those who need it,
        pray for others.
Enliven our hearts and guide our deeds.
In Jesus' name we pray.
Amen

Thirty-Third Sunday in Ordinary Time

Risk Security in Using Gifts Well

Invitation to Pray
Pause for a few moments of silence and enter more deeply into the presence of God.

> *Song:* "Christ, Be Our Light," Bernadette Farrell

> *Proclaim the gospel:* Matthew 25:14-30
> "Well Done, My Good and Faithful Servant."

Take a few minutes to savour a word, a phrase, a question, or a feeling that rises up in you. Reflect on this quietly or share it aloud.

Invitation to Reflect
The parables of Jesus in this, his last major set of instructions found in Matthew's Gospel, are rich with meaning for us, both individually and as a Church. In this particular parable of the talents, we who live in the 'in-between' time, waiting for the fullness of God's reign, are reminded that we are to live in harmony with the earth. The treasures of the earth, the gifts of the Holy Spirit, and the charisms of the Church are in our safekeeping. The question that is set before us is, "Will we risk failure or even loss to increase the treasure trove of God's abundance?"

The talent, or Greek *talanton*, referred to in the gospel was a huge monetary silver coin that represented a lifetime of earnings. The first servant had five lifetimes of earnings, the next had two, and the third servant was responsible for one lifetime of earnings. More importantly, this reminds us of the generous abundance of God. We all are blessed with a treasure of gifts and graces that flow unearned into our daily lives. We, the Church, are abundantly blessed and gifted to bring forth the reign of God—that state of justice, peace, and communion for which we all long. In a culture that continually preys upon our fears, the myth of scarcity prevails. We do not have enough money, time, or resources. But Jesus continually reminds us, from the feeding of the crowds to this parable of the talents, that God's generosity will not be outdone.

Furthermore, the question of stewardship over such a huge treasure is vital to God's plan. The servant to whom the master gave the least treasure to tend feared the master, and even more, feared failure. He could not risk allowing the talent to grow and multiply, so he buried it. Burying, hoarding, and stubborn clinging to what is freely given was adamantly condemned by Jesus. How can we hang on to what was not ours in the first place? The gifts, the talents are given to be used for the sake of the whole. We all possess a multitude of charisms or gifts, entrusted to us by the graciousness of God. For our part, we must develop them, generously offering them for the benefit of the community of humankind and the earth. The Church, too, is abundantly blessed. We, who are the Church, must see to it that these blessings pour over into society to benefit all of creation.

The reward for such generous self-giving is to be given even greater responsibility. We can never think our task is complete. We are asked to do and to be even more, so that our circle of influence will grow larger and larger. Look at the simple gesture of compassion toward one dying person that was the only goal of Mother Teresa. She never tried to change whole systems of poverty; her only mission was to be with one person at a time. Yet her circle of influence affected the whole world.

Invitation to Group Sharing

1. What does this parable say about my current spiritual growth? What changes do I need to make in my life?

2. How rich in treasure and talent are those in my group? What are some talents I can name for each person present?

3. Look at the rich treasure of the Church community in which you worship. What are some treasures that are being given for the benefit of the whole parish? The larger social community?

4. What are some of the obstacles that keep me and others in our group from fully giving of our time and talent? What will I or we do to overcome these obstacles?

Invitation to Act

Determine a specific action (individual or group) that flows from your sharing. This should be your primary consideration. When choosing an individual action, determine what you will do and share it with the group. When choosing a group action, determine who will take responsibility for different aspects of the action. The following are secondary suggestions:

1. Take an inventory of the gifts you have used in the past year. From these determine some action you can take to further develop the gifts you have been given.

2. Name the fears that keep you from offering your gifts to the parish or your social community. Pray each day this week to overcome these fears, remembering that fear of the Lord, that is, awe for God's generosity, erases human fear.

3. In your group, take time to name your charisms, affirm one another in the gifts you see, and encourage one another in using these talents to meet the needs of others.

4. Look at the wonders of creation together by taking a walk or having a picnic. Name and give thanks for the gifts of the earth that are in our safekeeping. Determine how you will be in better relationship with the earth.

5. Reflect on the gifts of a family member, a friend, a colleague, or a neighbour. Pray for that person.

Invitation to Closing Prayer
Give thanks to God (aloud or silently) for insights gained, for desires awakened, for directions clarified, for the gift of one another's openness and sensitivity. Conclude with the following:

Generous God, you have
    blessed us with abundant treasures.
We offer our thanks for your graciousness
    by naming and claiming these gifts together.

Begin a litany of thanks, using the following phrase to initiate the naming of these gifts:
"I acknowledge your gift of _____ in my life. Give me the grace me to use this talent for the benefit of others."

When all have finished, close with the following words:
May your kingdom come.
    May your will be done as we offer these gifts for the sake of all.
    Amen

Last Sunday in Ordinary Time
OUR LORD JESUS CHRIST, UNIVERSAL KING

Selfless Love Is the Sign of Christ's Reign

Invitation to Pray
Pause for a few moments of silence and enter more deeply into the presence of God.

> ***Song:*** "Hail Redeemer, King Divine," Patrick Brennan CSsR

> ***Proclaim the gospel:*** Matthew 25:31-46
> "Whatever You Did…You Did for Me."

Take a few minutes to savour a word, a phrase, a question, or a feeling that rises up in you. Reflect on this quietly or share it aloud.

Invitation to Reflect
Separating sheep from goats was a familiar routine for the shepherds in Jesus' day. Each night, the mixed herds would have to be separated. The hardy sheep could sleep outdoors in the cold Palestinian evenings, while the goats had to be sheltered for warmth. Today's passage is yet another story on divine judgment. Matthew's Gospel is peppered with images of separating: weeds from wheat, fish in the dragnet, trees that bear fruit from trees that are barren, wedding guests with garments from those without, and good servants from abusive ones. The most striking thing about today's separation of goats and sheep is that Matthew introduces this with the words, "When the Son of Man comes in his glory…he will sit upon his glorious throne" (v. 31). These words signify the final separating, the glory of Jesus' kingship over all, and the judgment of the nations by the shepherd-king.

Judgment—the separating of the nations—is left to the harvest time, the end time, by the shepherd-king who judges with a focus upon the basis of loving the "least." The least are those in need. Simple acts of love, kindness, and compassion are required of humankind. In these simple acts of providing food, water, clothing, shelter, company and solace, the believer discovers the presence of Christ who reigns in the hearts of all people. These small, somewhat insignificant deeds have eternal implications upon which we shall be judged in the end time.

Only active, overflowing love can prepare for the reign of Christ the King. The caring, seeking, and embracing love of the shepherd for his flock characterises this kingship. Thus, the circle of love and care for others is the only way to unleash the kingdom, the reign of Christ the King, in this time and place. Care and compassion toward one another are the actions whereby Jesus' authority and power are exerted over humankind today. As followers of Jesus, we are moved to honour our king by the simple deeds of love that witness the power of God's kingdom.

Invitation to Group Sharing

1. As I reflect upon this passage, what do I find the most challenging?

2. Together determine the many ways people are hungry, thirsty, naked, imprisoned, or sick. How have I tried to meet these material, emotional, and spiritual needs in the past?

3. What are some ways our parish community and our local community meet these simple needs of the least in our midst?

4. How can I engage more effectively in sharing God's love?

Invitation to Act

Determine a specific action (individual or group) that flows from your sharing. This should be your primary consideration. When choosing an individual action, determine what you will do and share it with the group. When choosing a group action, determine who will take responsibility for different aspects of the action. The following are secondary suggestions:

1. Share your love with one person this week.

2. Visit the housebound in your neighbourhood, bringing them food, laughter and your company.

3. Offer your time and talents to prepare someone for a job, to assist with budgeting, or to share your skills with someone in need. If there is transitional housing in or near your community, you may find someone in need there.

4. Sponsor a refugee family in your parish by providing clothing, jobs, housing, and household items.

5. Spend a few minutes each night in prayerful gratitude for those who have shown kindness to you throughout the day.

Invitation to Closing Prayer
Give thanks to God (aloud or silently) for insights gained, for desires awakened, for directions clarified, for the gift of one another's openness and sensitivity. Conclude with the following:

Christ, our King,
    grant that we will see you in
    the eyes of the poor and sick,
    those who are disregarded in our society.
We ask, too, that these, the least among us,
    might find you in our simple deeds of love.
May we be your eyes and ears,
        your feet and arms,
        your loving embrace to all we meet.
We ask this under the grace of your Holy Spirit in the
        power of your kingship. Amen

Music Resources

All of the music resources suggested in this publication can be found in common hymn books such as:

Laudate

Celebration Hymnal for Everyone

Liturgical Calendar

Year A	2005		2008	
1st Sunday of Advent	Nov. 28, 2004		Dec. 2, 2007	
2nd Sunday of Advent	Dec.	5	Dec.	9
3rd Sunday of Advent	Dec.	12	Dec.	16
4th Sunday of Advent	Dec.	19	Dec.	23
Holy Family	Dec.	26	Dec.	30
Mary, Mother of God, Jan. 1	Saturday		Tuesday	
Epiphany	Jan. 6, 2005		Jan. 6, 2008	
Baptism of the Lord	Jan.	9	Jan.	13
2nd Sunday in Ordinary Time	Jan.	16	Jan.	20
3rd Sunday in Ordinary Time	Jan.	23	Jan.	27
4th Sunday in Ordinary Time	Jan.	30	Feb.	3
5th Sunday in Ordinary Time	Feb.	6	—	
6th Sunday in Ordinary Time	—	—	—	
7th Sunday in Ordinary Time	—	—	—	
8th Sunday in Ordinary Time	—	—	—	
1st Sunday of Lent	Feb.	13	Feb.	10
2nd Sunday of Lent	Feb.	20	Feb.	17
3rd Sunday of Lent	Feb.	27	Feb.	24
4th Sunday of Lent	Mar.	6	Mar.	2
5th Sunday of Lent	Mar.	13	Mar.	9
Palm Sun. of the Lord's Passion	Mar.	20	Mar.	16
Easter	Mar.	27	Mar.	23
2nd Sunday of Easter	Apr.	3	Mar.	30
3rd Sunday of Easter	Apr.	10	Apr.	6
4th Sunday of Easter	Apr.	17	Apr.	13
5th Sunday of Easter	Apr.	24	Apr.	20
6th Sunday of Easter	May	1	Apr.	27
Ascension +	May	5	May	1
7th Sunday of Easter	May	8	May	4
Pentecost	May	15	May	11
Trinity Sunday	May	22	May	18
Body and Blood of Christ	May	26	May	22

Year A	2005		2008	
9th Sunday in Ordinary Time	— — —	—	June	1
10th Sunday in Ordinary Time	June	5	June	8
11th Sunday in Ordinary Time	June	12	June	15
12th Sunday in Ordinary Time	June	19	June	22
13th Sunday in Ordinary Time	June	26	—	
14th Sunday in Ordinary Time	July	3	July	6
15th Sunday in Ordinary Time	July	10	July	13
16th Sunday in Ordinary Time	July	17	July	20
17th Sunday in Ordinary Time	July	24	July	27
18th Sunday in Ordinary Time	July	31	Aug.	3
19th Sunday in Ordinary Time	Aug.	7	Aug.	10
20th Sunday in Ordinary Time	Aug.	14	Aug.	17
21st Sunday in Ordinary Time	Aug.	21	Aug.	24
22nd Sunday in Ordinary Time	Aug.	28	Aug.	31
23rd Sunday in Ordinary Time	Sept.	4	Sept.	7
24th Sunday in Ordinary Time	Sept.	11	—	
25th Sunday in Ordinary Time	Sept.	18	Sept.	21
26th Sunday in Ordinary Time	Sept.	25	Sept.	28
27th Sunday in Ordinary Time	Oct.	2	Oct.	5
28th Sunday in Ordinary Time	Oct.	9	Oct.	12
29th Sunday in Ordinary Time	Oct.	16	Oct.	19
30th Sunday in Ordinary Time	Oct.	23	Oct.	26
31st Sunday in Ordinary Time	Oct.	30	—	
32nd Sunday in Ordinary Time	Nov.	6	—	
33rd Sunday in Ordinary Time	Nov.	13	Nov.	16
Christ the King	Nov.	20	Nov.	23